The Complete
Predator Hunter

Mike Schoby

©2009 Michael Schoby

Published by

krause publications
A subsidiary of F+W Media, Inc.

700 East State Street • Iola, WI 54990-0001
715-445-2214 • 888-457-2873
www.krausebooks.com

Our toll-free number to place an order or obtain
a free catalog is (800) 258-0929.

Library of Congress Control Number: 2009923227

ISBN-13: 978-0-89689-937-7
ISBN-10: 0-89689-937-3

Designed by Al West
Edited by Corrina Peterson

Printed in China

DEDICATION

To the folks who keep reading my material, thank you for allowing me to avoid a real job.

ACKNOWLEDGEMENTS

It is always hard to write a proper Acknowledgement chapter, for you know you will leave someone (if not several folks) out, as putting a book together is a big project that takes a lot of help from many sources. Whomever I forgot I apologize in advance for my faulty memory.

To start with I need to thank Mark Zepp who has been a good friend, mentor, videographer and long-time, but too infrequent hunting companion. He is to credit for the excellent video work. Hopefully we will be able to spend more time in the field together going forward.

I also need to thank Doug Howlett, Jeff Hughes, Derrek Sigler, and Ralph Lermayer who not only do I consider good friends, but great industry professionals who have always made my work much better.

Finally a tip of the cap to my brother Greg Schoby who has turned into an obsessed-lunatic predator hunter, as well as the old Washington hunting crew of Mike Lunenschloss, Taro Sakita, Todd Eldred and Mark Torres who are always more than willing to grab a call and go hunting as well as providing me many photos when I get thin.

C O N T E N T S

PASSING IT ON

By Ralph Lermayer

A long time ago, a scrubby 12-year-old boy, hunkered down behind a log jam in New York's Catskill Mountains, blew an unrecognizable wail from a discarded clarinet mouthpiece. He had no success in previous attempts at this odd exercise, but a dog-eared magazine article told him it could happen.

Then, as if by magic, he found himself eyeball to eyeball with a ferocious (to a 12-year-old) red fox. That standoff lasted mere seconds, but it launched a lifetime passion for calling predators that drives his life – my life – to this day.

We've come a long way from the days when a mouth call was all we needed. Today, there's high tech new gear available that we never dreamed possible. Remote controlled, wireless electronic calls can be set up far from the shooter. Units not only deliver high fidelity, but let you remotely control moving decoys. Even the wind is closer to doing our bidding, as the newest units can send out a burst of "confusion scent" at the push of a button. Open reed mouth calls are now so simple to use anyone who can blow out the candles on a birthday cake can deliver howls, locators, estrus chirps and come-hither sounds. New camo and an array of lifelike decoys drop the guard of predators from the meekest to the baddest.

It's all at your fingertips, all you need is the right person to put it together and explain the tactics to make you successful. The book you hold in your hand does just that. I've known Mike Schoby for many years, as both a friend and a contributor to *Predator Xtreme* magazine. Authors that appear in *PX* must be predator hunters first, solidly grounded in experience, and have something beneficial to share with readers in a way they can understand. Mike Schoby is precisely that kind of author. He has been there, done it all, and has valuable advice to offer the novice or the pro.

You have the gear, there are plenty of coyotes, now sit back and a let a real predator hunter tell you how to put it all together. Enjoy this book. You've chosen your mentor well.

Hunt hard, shoot straight, kill clean and apologize to no one.
Ralph M. Lermayer
Editor, Predator Xtreme magazine

Enjoying the challenge, *just being there, and witnessing a fantastic sunrise are all part of why we predator hunt.*

CHAPTER

1

WHY WE HUNT PREDATORS

Iam often asked, by people who don't hunt predators, why I do. In answer, more often than not I rely on the old line, "If I have to explain it you wouldn't understand." Indeed, this vague answer works in many situations. I've used it to justify more rifle purchases and to try explaining why I hunt, fish and enjoy the outdoors. I've even used it to defend bringing another mount into the house. The bottom line is that sometimes it's hard to put feelings into words. Sometimes it's just easier to say "You wouldn't understand" than to really express the reason we do something.

Do I have a rational reason for hunting predators? Can a logical financial argument be made for spending hundreds, even thousands, of dollars to obtain a pelt worth possibly fifty bucks (in a good year)? Probably not, especially considering I haven't sold a pelt since I was in college when $25 went a long way in beer and pizza. Anymore I generally send off the pelts to a tannery and spend another $25 or so getting them tanned to add to my already too cluttered den. So if its not money, what is it?

The argument can be made that hunting predators is good game management. The old adage of "kill a coyote save a (insert whatever game species you want here, such as pheasant, or quail or deer)" is popular among sportsmen. But does predator hunting really help game populations? I like to think so, but the scientific evidence doesn't strongly support the claim.

So, what other reasons could there be for hunting predators? For meat, possibly? Not hardly. While I have attempted eating a coyote once to prove a point, stocking the larder with fresh coyote meat is definitely not the reason I hunt them.

> Why do I spend way too much money on new rifles, gas for the pickup, cold weather clothing and specialty ammunition for something I can't eat anyway?

After considering all the standard reasons for hunting predators and eliminating them one by one, I'm still left with the question: Why? Why do I spend countless hours freezing in the winter and roasting in the summer? Why do I spend way too much money on new rifles, gas for the pickup, cold weather clothing and specialty ammunition for something I can't eat anyway? If predators are not helping or hurting the game population one way or the other, as a sportsman do I really care? Why *do* I hunt them day after day, season after season and year after year?

I guess the short answer is simply because I love the whole experience. I love hearing that lone howl echo off the canyon walls in the early morning stillness. I love seeing a coyote sneaking through the sage. I'm fascinated by their fur blowing in the wind. And I admit that I enjoy squeezing the trigger when they finally get in range.

Beyond that, I like a challenge and with predators I "lose" far more often then I "win." When I head afield, even with the most modern advances in rifles, calls, optics and decoys, a coyote still has a better chance of seeing me, smelling me or having a sixth sense tell him there's a rat in the woodpile. If predator hunting were easy, like shooting prairie dogs, you can bet I wouldn't be as enthralled with it as I am. I may do it once a year (much like prairie dog shooting), but if it was *just* about pulling the trigger, you can rest assured I wouldn't be that excited about it.

The challenge is what makes it fun. There is a sense of satisfaction in knowing you can on occasion fool them. Not everyone can, at least not regularly. To regularly put fur on the stretcher you must have a bit of know-how in the hunting skills department. This is probably more true for predators than for any other animal we hunt in North America. You are truly hunting the hunter.

Predator hunting *is one way to spend time outdoors with family and friends.*

Consider this: If deer could be hunted year around, 24 hours a day with no limit, few equipment restrictions and without even a license, how long would it take before they were declared endangered? Now factor in a handful of government agents in each state using any means necessary to hunt the animals, including poison and aircraft. I'd say deer would be endangered in less than ten years. Considering the fact that most predators, especially coyotes, are "managed" under these criteria and their population is thriving, I would say as a hunter you have found an ultimate challenge.

Humans are driven by challenges. Success over obstacles and hurdles is what keeps many of us moving forward. We need a stick with which to measure ourselves, and the occasional challenge provides it. This is why some climb mountains, run marathons or even play golf - because of the inherent difficulty of the act. This is no different than why I hunt predators.

So head afield, meet the challenge and participate in possibly the greatest game available to hunters...the calling of predators.

CHAPTER

2

NEW GEAR FOR PREDATOR HUNTERS

I t is tough talking about new gear in terms of predator hunting, as the sport is growing in leaps and bounds. It seems like every time I turn around there is something new on the market specifically for predator hunters. Some of the stuff is excellent, some is good and some is a gimmicky waste of time. This chapter presents only the products I feel fall into the good or excellent category. These are the products I use and like and would recommend to friends.

One of the beautiful things about predator hunting in our increasingly costly world is that, boiled down to its essence, predator hunting is still a cheap sport. There are no fancy leases for predators, few guided hunts and no license requirements in some states. You can still put on a pair of tan jeans and a brown checked flannel shirt, slip a five dollar call in your pocket and head afield with any rifle you may have in your collection. Odds are, such equipped, you will still kill your fair share of predators if you know how to do it.

Because of this, new gear is not necessary, but in some cases adding gear to your collection may make you more effective and a lot of the time more comfortable. If you like gear, read on. If not, skip ahead to other chapters.

Clothing

Since predators range over such a wide variety of real estate and seasons run year-round, selecting the right clothing is a bit more complicated than it might be for a white-tail deer hunter who only hunts the first two weeks of November. A predator hunter may find himself in waist deep snow in the mountains or sitting in the sand in the desert with the temperature soaring into triple digits – all within a few days time. For this reason, dressing in layers is mandatory for most predator hunting.

> For early fall in the North and year-round use in more moderate climates, one system I really like is the Sitka clothing system.

For early fall in the North and year-round use in more moderate climates, one system I really like is the Sitka clothing system. Starting with their Polartec base layer, followed by their Traverse insulating system and finally topped off with one of their various outer layers such as the 90% Series, you have a clothing system that can handle about any condition a predator hunter will face, from sitting in the Arizona desert to climbing mountains for cougars to hunting fox in the winter. It is easy to unzip the armpit zippers on the outer layer to increase ventilation and let moisture escape, or remove the insulating layer all

If you're hunting *in the dead of winter, it's especially important to select the right clothing.*

together if you get to hot. If the weather turns cold, the jacket can be zipped up and closed down, and yet another insulating layer can be added under the shell for additional warmth. This is the kind of flexibility that the right set of clothing provides.

For severe winter weather, I prefer to not only don more layers in a layering system, but to use an outer layer to visually match the surroundings. The Cabela's Canadian pant and jacket is a great choice since it goes over your normal hunting clothes. Bundle up with normal gear and, when the ground turns white, pull out the lightweight top and bottom and virtually disappear into your winter wonderland surroundings.

Packs

A pack is a handy tool for any predator hunter, especially one that has amassed so much stuff that jacket pockets will no longer handle it. A good pack serves many functions. It can haul bulky gear in and haul dead predators out. It can keep calls separate, silent and organized, ready for instant use. A really good pack will also carry a lunch and a thermos of coffee.

> A good pack serves many functions. It can haul bulky gear in and haul dead predators out.

Over the years I've used various pack designs, from small fanny packs to aluminum tubular frame packs. In recent years there have been some major improvements in pack design made specifically with the predator hunter in mind.

A predator pack has to be big enough to haul a moderate amount of gear, but not so big that it's cumbersome for the short day excursions predator hunters make. The average predator hunter is not heading afield with several days of provisions. If the pack has the means to carry a coyote or fox back to the truck, that's a bonus. If it has specialty storage, such as insulated or waterproof pockets for a GPS, rangefinder or camera, that's even better.

An ideal predator pack needs enough small compartments to keep gear such as knives and calls separate for organization as well as stealth. It also needs to be durable. Weak straps, poor quality zippers or inferior material that can't hold up to rugged use shouldn't be considered. A pack that is water/weather resistant is a big plus as predator hunters contend with rain or snow on a pretty regular basis, even in the desert.

While there are lots of great packs on the market today here are three of my favorites:

Black's Creek Predator Paradise

This is one unique, well made pack that is ideal for predator hunting. As the name implies, it has been designed from the ground up with predator killing in mind. Essentially, it is an oversized fanny pack with a shoulder strap system that is both comfortable and easy to get into and out of. The main compartment is specifically designed to carry a FOXPRO call and a FOXPRO Jack In The Box decoy. The side compartments are ideal for organizing smaller items like calls, cameras and radios.

The Predator Paradise comes complete with a well thought out, thick, padded seat cushion (designed to pull double duty as a shooting rest) that snaps to the pack for easy transport. It also provides a blood-proof bag and strap system for carrying predators back to the truck. With 1,400 cubic inches of storage, this is a great mid-sized pack. With the predator carrying system, it performs like a much larger pack.

Eberlestock Gunslinger

There are several features I like about the Eberlestock Gunslinger pack. To begin with, it's built military tough. Extra large straps, heavy duty buckles, quality fabric – in short, you would have to drag this pack behind a pickup for hundreds of miles before you could wear it out.

Next is its versatility. This pack can be compressed to be a regular-sized day pack or expanded for

While the Eberlestock Gunslinger pack works well for all types of predator hunting, it is also ideal for suburban hunters looking to stay under the radar.

Eberlestock
packs are fantastic for carrying your gear and your rifle into the field.

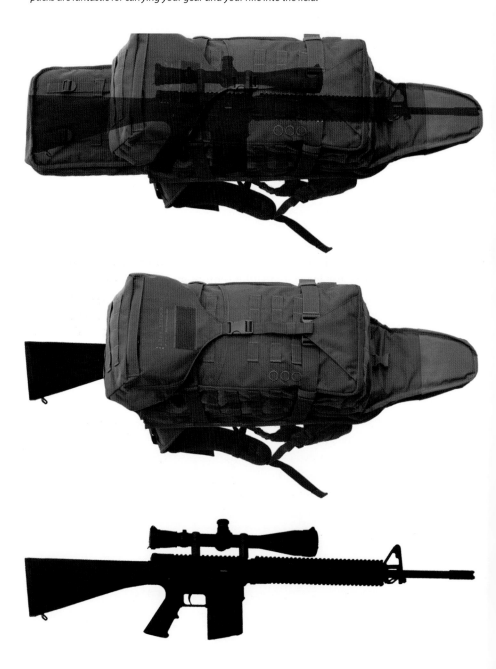

large "hauling out" capabilities. In addition to the rugged expandable design, I also really like the small features such as the full length side zipper, which is perfect for finding what you need at the bottom of the pack without removing everything from the top. With some judicial packing and a blood-proof plastic bag, the Gunslinger is also large enough to stuff a predator up to the size of a coyote inside.

While the Eberlestock Gunslinger pack works well for all types of predator hunting, it is also ideal for suburban hunters looking to stay under the radar. It has a built-in gun sleeve with a snaptop cover to completely hide any rifle.

Sitka Bivy

The Sitka Bivy is an ideal pack for the hunter who wants to own one pack for all types of hunting. The design allows it to be compressed down very small so it is not much bigger than a day pack. It can also be expanded to one monstrous load carrier for large items like remote megaphone speakers, coyote decoys or even packing out a predator carcass. To complement the versatility, the top of the pack snaps off and turns into an ideal calling fanny pack. Hunters could easily keep all of their calls and predator hunting accessories in the top compartment and choose to carry either the whole pack or just the fanny portion as the hunt dictates.

Another feature I like on the Sitka Bivy is the excellent support system. All of the packs mentioned here have great support systems, but from my experience the Bivy ranks right at the top. It is extremely comfortable and, best of all for hunters operating in warm weather, sports the best ventilation design of all the packs to keep the back cool and sweat-free.

Electronics

While I cover electronic calls for predator hunters in the calling chapter, there are other types of electronics available that are worth mentioning here. The items not only make hunters more successful, as is the case with GPS units, but often make the hunt more enjoyable and memorable, as with digital video cameras.

The Bushnell BackTrack *is a simple but effective GPS unit.*

GPS

A quality GPS unit is one of the first items a predator hunter should stow in the pack. While not always necessary for the hunter making stands just out of sight from the truck, it can become a lifesaver for hunters heading deep into the backcountry or venturing out on foot for an all day hike through the desert. In open country it is often easy enough to see landmarks, but that is not always the case. If an overcast day settles in or a snow storm picks up, it is not uncommon to get turned around and become disoriented.

In addition to the safety aspect of a GPS, more advanced units are also an excellent tool for marking good calling stands. I'm constantly amazed at how forgetful I can be. I've hunted areas before that turned out to be excellent, but for

> In addition to the safety aspect of a GPS, more advanced units are also an excellent tool for marking good calling stands.

whatever reason may not return to that spot for a couple of years. When I do return, I sometimes have a hard time remembering which road I went in on, where I made a stand and in which order I should hit stands for the best success. When you mark a spot on a GPS, it's easy to return year after year, regardless of how your memory works.

There are many GPS units to choose from. Two of my favorites are the Garmin Etrex series and the newly released Bushnell Onix 400. The Etrex models come in several configurations from extremely simple to as complex as you want to get. The Bushnell Onix has a full-color, extremely large display screen with complete topographics and satellite photography.

If you are not technologically-oriented, take a look at Bushnell's newest GPS unit, the BackTrack. Instead of being built with every conceivable function under the sun, Bushnell made about as simple as you can get. With a push of a button it will take you back to your vehicle or up to three previously marked locations. The BackTrack is ideal for keeping in your pack as a backup GPS or just in your pocket for those rare times when you become temporarily disoriented.

> The BackTrack is ideal for keeping in your pack as a backup GPS or just in your pocket for those rare times when you become temporarily disoriented.

Lights

Lighting is the next important item for a predator hunter's pack. I generally keep one of two kinds of lights: a high intensity flashlight such as a SureFire or an Insight for general navigation at night as well as limited night shooting. I have used these flashlights on several continents and am very pleased with both. Both are well made, durable with a capital "D" and super bright. Of the two, I tend to prefer the Insight as it is a high-tech, programmable flashlight with an auto shut off function and several intensity settings. The first feature ensures it doesn't turn on in my pack, wearing out the batteries before I need it, and the second function is ideal for getting just the right amount of light: low intensity for loading a gun or reading a map, medium intensity for walking into a calling stand and high

> Both (SureFire and Insight) are well made, durable with a capital "D" and super bright.

intensity for occasional night hunting.

In addition to one of these quality flashlights, I also pack a dedicated gun-mounted spotlight for night hunting. For night hunting lights, I currently own a Midnight Lite and a Lightforce. Both are excellent, with a slight nod in power going to the Lightforce but a vote for compactness going to the Midnight Lite.

Radios

Aside from flashlights and a GPS unit, I like to keep a pair of handheld radios in my pack. These come in handy when two hunters want to split up and still be able to communicate. While I don't use them on every stand, they have come down so much in price and are so user friendly there is really no reason not to own a set, even if you only use them once a year. There are many affordable, quality units available from several manufacturers.

Video Cameras

The final electronic device a predator hunter should consider purchasing is a micro digital video camera. These units are pretty handy for capturing the moment. The two units I have used the most are the Bushnell Videoscope and the Stealth Cam Epic. Both capture short video clips in an easily downloadable format and can be mounted to a gun. Of the two, the Bushnell in my opinion is more user friendly when mounted on a gun, but the Epic has the advantage of easily adapting to other purposes such as a bow or head mount. Keep in mind you won't be shooting any cinematic masterpieces with either camera as the quality of the footage is relatively low, but they are ideal for making home movies and sharing footage from the field with friends over the Internet.

> When you buy optics, buy the best you can afford. There is a big difference between good and bad in this market.

Good binoculars
*like these Nikons,
help you see more
predators. Keeping
them clean also helps
considerably.*

Optics

You can hunt predators without good binoculars, as I did for years, and be successful. However, with them you will definitely do much better. It's amazing how many more coyotes you will see with binoculars than you will without them, especially out West where the distances are great. A set of ears coming through the sage, or a bobcat's eyes peering through a patch of Russian olive trees just pops out, even though you looked at the same spot just seconds before without binoculars.

When you buy optics, buy the best you can afford. There is a big difference between good and bad in this market. Good optics are a joy to hunt with and allow you to use them for hours on end. Bad optics are miserable to use and will give you a headache after minutes of using them. Take my advice on this one, you are better to do without for a year or so and save up to buy quality than spend your money early on an inferior set of glass.

You don't have to get too high of a magnification for predator hunting. In fact, I prefer lower powered models. For predator hunting you are not trying to determine trophy size as you are with so many other species. More often than not, the species in question is on the move, making them much easier to see than say a mule deer buck bedded in the shadows of a juniper. Lower-powered optics also give you a better field of view (you will cover more area at a time) and better light transmitting abilities.

I use the Nikon Premier binocular quite a bit when predator hunting. It is light, compact and has excellent glass, rivaling that of many renowned European manufacturers.

> I have owned probably every model Harris makes and have fitted them to many different types of rifles over the years. The reason I used them in the beginning and still use them today is because they work.

Shooting Supports

No matter how good a shot you are, a shooting support aid of some type will increase your hit ratio on small-framed predators such as coyotes and fox. Over the years I've used several types of these supports, but now have my favorites narrowed down to the following:

Harris BiPod

I'll bet I've had a Harris Bipod attached to at least one predator rifle for the last 20 years. I have owned probably every model Harris makes and have fitted them to many different types of rifles over the years. The reason I used them in the beginning and still use them today is because they work. They are rock solid and always at hand. Of all the models they make, I now generally only use one, the Model 25C, which is the tallest of the Harris bipods. Its three-piece leg construction is adjustable from 13½ inches to 27 inches with a swiveling top. This model is ideal for sitting, which I do the majority of the time for predators, and the swiveling function is mandatory. While it is possible to level a rifle with a fixed Harris bipod, the swivel makes the job much easier. The only downside to the Harris bipod is the fact that they are relatively heavy and can get in the way if you need to pick up the rifle for a running shot.

Photo courtesy Harris Engineering, Inc.

Sniper Styx

The Sniper Styx come in several varieties – from tripods to more traditional bipods – with an assortment of different foot attachments and extensions. Basically, they are extruded aluminum poles attached at the top with a rubber yoke which forms a cradle for the gun. The legs themselves are available either in black or dipped in Mossy Oak Brush camo. What I like about these units is that they are super lightweight, quiet and versatile. The original model can be used at a variety of heights and shooting positions, and it is easy to pick up the rifle if a coyote comes in close and a running or moving shot is anticipated.

Photo courtesy Predator Sniper Products

CHAPTER 3

ADVANCED DECOYS FOR PREDATOR HUNTERS

T he first time I used a decoy I was 15 years old. I affixed a stiff, salt-cured rabbit skin to an old arrow shaft with some fishing line. If there was sufficient breeze, the skin would flop around and look somewhat lifelike (at least as lifelike as a salt-cured rabbit skin, prepared by a 15-year-old, can look).

On one set, I remember placing the decoy out in front of me 50 yards before I started to call. Within about six minutes I heard rocks rolling behind my left shoulder. Not wanting to turn completely around, I snuck a glance over my shoulder and was amazed to see not one but two coyotes stealthily working their way toward the decoy. In no position to take a shot, I quit making any sounds and let them come the rest of the way to the decoy on sight alone. They snuck in, their attention fixated on the decoy the entire time. When they got close enough to smell it they realized it wasn't a live rabbit, but by then it was too late. I was already aiming down on the first coyote. At the crack of the rifle my mind turned to a coveted double. Both coyotes took off up the hillside. Either my gun was off or I got a touch of coyote fever. But even though I didn't have a dead coyote to show for it, I was convinced of the effectiveness of decoys.

Decoys can't make a bad set right or magically make predators appear, but they help tip the odds a little in a predator hunter's favor, especially when you need something to draw a predators attention to give you a good shot. Keep in mind, I don't use them on every set. Sometimes they are not needed and, in really open country, the act of setting them up may even spook predators. If you are calling in open country (Nebraska and eastern Colorado come to mind) it is darn tough to stay hidden from coyotes. When you set up, more often than not a coyote is within view and any extra movement may alert him to your presence.

This is why, when hunting this type of country, I generally sneak to an elevated position, crest the top (often lying prone) and start calling. If you crest the ridge and work down the other side 50 yards to put up a decoy, you would spook more coyotes than you would lure in. In my opinion, a decoy is a must-have in every pack, but it is not necessary a must-use on every set. That being said, when the country is right and a decoy is used in conjunction with a remote electronic caller, it increases the odds that you will get a clean, unhurried shot.

Since so many hunters now realize the effectiveness of decoys, they now come in all shapes and sizes – from lifelike recreations of real prey to stylistic impressions of something furred or feathered and edible. From wind operated to battery powered, to decoys so advanced they are activated by noise and choreographed to calling sequences, there is something for everyone. Even before I started testing this latest crop of decoys I knew they all had one thing in common: They all could fool a predator in the right situation. So the real question is, which ones perform best for a hunter under field conditions? Which are easiest to carry afield, simple enough to set up in cold weather, rugged enough to last season after season, and offer good value for the money? Which ones can be seen the greatest distance? These are the criteria I used to review currently available predator decoys.

> Since so many hunters now realize the effectiveness of decoys, they now come in all shapes and sizes – from lifelike recreations of real prey to stylistic impressions of something furred or feathered and edible.

Coyote Decoys

Coyote decoys have come into their own in the last few years with the increased popularity among hunters using coyote vocalization. Unlike a prey decoy that works any time of the year, predator decoys may only work well during specific seasons.

The best time to use a predator decoy is when the mating and denning season is at its peak. As a rule of thumb, when coyotes become territorial and start responding to howling, a predator decoy should be thrown in the mix. However, like any decoy that could be mistaken for the real thing, be careful how and where you use them. If there is a chance there could be other hunters in the area, use caution when using a coyote decoy. Make sure you set up and position yourself so you can see all angles of approach and keep a safe zone – such as a rock pile or large tree – at your back in case a hunter mistakes your decoy for the real thing and sneaks in to your calling. It is also not a bad idea to keep the decoy in a hunter orange bag when transporting into and out of the field. Don't be afraid of using a predator decoy, just follow the same precautions turkey hunters across America do every spring.

Flambeau Lone Howler

The Flambeau Lone Howler is a very realistic recreation of an adult coyote. Its hard-molded body design is well built and to scale. In addition to looking good, the Lone Howler has some unique features. To begin with, the leg sections are not permanently attached to the body. Instead, they snap into place and are held there by rubber shock cords. This serves two valuable functions. First, for transport the legs can be folded under the body and secured with the blaze orange carrying strap (included). Once in the field, with the moveable legs, the hunter can either have the coyote standing or sitting on his haunches. The hard body combined with the realistic soft tail makes for an overall awesome decoy that works very well.

Flambeau's Lone Howler *is a realistic decoy for hunters looking to challenge a coyote's territory. The legs fold up, which allows for easy transport and custom positioning.*

The Edge 'Yote
*looks realistic and is
easy to transport.*

Edge 'Yote Decoy

The 'Yote by Edge is a flexible, collapsible design which, like most all collapsible decoys, makes the challenge of transporting it afield an easier proposition. The lifelike soft tail imparts good movement in a breeze and is easily removable for storage between sets. While I felt the decoy was realistic enough looking and easy to transport, I have found that collapsible decoys don't always work well for me. The stakes can be tough to insert into rocky or hard ground and, as in the case of the 'Yote, the body has a tendency to fold upon itself and collapse while set up. However, it was nothing that a short stick or old arrow shaft inserted in the right place wouldn't fix.

Renzo Fox and Coyote

The Renzo line of digitally printed, silhouette decoys look extremely lifelike to my eyes. However, I don't know how they look to predators. For color-sighted game species like turkeys, ducks and geese, I have used the corresponding Renzo decoy and they work excellent. I'm just not sure how coyotes see them. My unscientific guess is they work just fine. To test this theory I set up the Renzo coyote in the back yard and let my dog out of the house. He saw it and went nuts; barking, hair bristling and growling. So as far as canine eyesight in general is concerned, the Renzo coyote is seen easily enough.

The Renzo
decoy is extremely lifelike. Best of all, it folds up into a small package for easy transport to and from the field.

As long as it works as well on coyotes as it does on Fido, the Renzo has the unique advantage of being the easiest of all predator decoys to transport afield. Remove the two metal stakes (which by the way were very easy to insert into even hard ground due to their small diameter) and fold the decoy on to itself. The decoy weighs mere ounces and can be strapped to the back of a predator pack.

Prey Decoys

Now comes a discussion of the meat and potatoes of the predator hunter's arsenal...prey decoys. A prey decoy gives predators the confidence that something worth eating is in the area. These decoys range from ultra-realistic mounts of specific game to mere suggestions of something small and edible. As far as effectiveness, I am more concerned with

In arid or rocky parts of the West, inserting a stake-type decoy can be difficult. Using the softer dirt of an ant mound can sometimes help to gain purchase.

rugged durability, long range appeal and ease of use over exact realism of prey. It has been my experience that predators are just as convinced with a suggestion of an animal as they are with an exact replica. I have also not seen any evidence that one type of decoy works better in one region of the country than another - they all seem to be universally effective.

> I have also not seen any evidence that one type of decoy works better in one region of the country than another - they all seem to be universally effective.

While the actual type of decoy remains effective from coast to coast, it is nice to be able to change a decoy's color to give it added visual attraction in different terrain or in snow cover. It is easier to do this with some decoys than others. Here are some of the more effective models on the market today.

Mojo Critter

This is a great example of an impressionistic decoy. The Mojo Critter looks like nothing in particular but is sure to get a response from hungry predators. What I like best about this decoy is that its long top section is easy to see from a distance. The intermittent movement also gives this decoy a touch of realism that I prefer over predictable, constant movement. The unit is well built with a solid steel stake system that works in even the hardest ground. While all stake supports will eventually meet their match in really rocky ground, this one is the toughest I've tested by far. I ran this unit for hours on the four AA batteries with no sign of it slowing down.

FOXPRO Jack In The Box

As one would expect from FOXPRO, this decoy is exceptionally well made, innovative and packed full of features. Built around a weather resistant molded plastic box (hence the name) which serves as its own base, there's no need for a stake, which I like. The decoy stores inside the box until the hunter is ready to use it.

When the ground
*is frozen solid, decoys
with bases, like this
Jack In The Box by
FOXPRO, are far
superior to stake-style
decoys*

While the batteries and electronics remain inside the box, the coolest aspect of this call is the control of the various settings which are easily accessed on the outside with switches. Hunters can choose delay, speed, remote and sound activated options as well as turn on a small LED light which illuminates the decoy.

Another feature I really liked is the option to easily replace the fuzzy decoy with factory units in different colors. Users could even make their own with what ever color they desire.

Renzo Rabbit

Like the Renzo fox and coyote decoy, their rabbit looks very lifelike (a bit more like a 4H Lop than a cottontail, but lifelike nonetheless). It is small and easily carried. However, I'm not sure how well it can be seen by a predator. To begin with, there is no movement with this decoy. Further, its diminutive size and height combined with its natural brown color make it hard to pick out at any distance. This decoy could be easily improved upon by a hunter at home with the addition of a feather or other moveable object, such as a piece of tissue paper affixed to the top with a tack or a spot of hot glue.

POWER SOLUTIONS

Regardless of the type of decoy you get, keep a few extra sets of batteries in your pack. It seems that Murphy is alive and well in the predator fields. Batteries will run out at the most inopportune time and one thing you can count on is no store in the immediate area to buy new ones. If the batteries are small like 9 volt, AA or AAA, I place several together in a vacuum bag and seal them up. This keeps them from getting wet and, in the event that they start to seep acid if you forget them in the bottom of the pack for a few years, it won't get all over your stuff. Best of all, when sealed in a vacuum bag they don't rattle around against other gear, making excess noise.

Edge Prowler Bait and Caller

The Edge Prowler Bait and Caller *emits the chirping sound of a bird in distress, and the plastic bird moves in conjunction with the sound.*

This diminutive call/decoy is designed more as an active bait for trapping than it is for predator calling. However, I think it would work well for specialty calling situations – particularly for bobcats and possibly red fox, especially in dense wooded cover where animals are apt to be close before seen. The base unit emits a high-pitched, chirping sound of a bird in distress and the plastic injection-molded bird on top moves in conjunction with the sound. At only several inches tall, this unit would have to be used in the right area (like set on a rock pile). With separate, louder calling, but for the final approach of a bobcat, I think it would fix their attention long enough for a hunter to get a shot.

Flambeau Rigor Rabbit

This decoy has probably been around the longest of all commercially-made predator decoys. It is molded from soft foam and sits on an unbalanced base to create movement. While it does work, and I personally had success with it years ago on coyotes, the design is rather basic and self limiting. It does not have intermittent movement, react to sound or feature replaceable covers. In addition, the movement it does have is not nearly as much as some of the other designs tested. And while it does look realistic to the human eye (especially up close), my unscientific guess is that – much like the difference between a Wooley Bugger and molded plastic cricket for the trout fisherman – a more impressionistic, furry decoy probably has more appeal at longer distances to predators.

Mojo Woodpecker

This is a great decoy, especially in light of recent studies on predator vision. While I don't think woodpeckers comprise a large portion of any predator's diet, coyotes, fox and bobcats – being opportunists – do eat them, especially when the birds are wounded and easy to catch. But more important than their status as food is their coloring. Bold black, red and white markings can be seen from quite a distance, which makes them especially susceptible to predator vision.

This decoy can be run with both wings affixed or, as I like to run it, with only one wing in place giving it the look of an injured woodpecker. The metal stake is sturdy and easy to insert into hard ground. For a more versatile presentation, the integrated loop on top of the head allows it to be suspended from a branch or fence wire.

Edge Wounded Woodpecker

The Edge Wounded Woodpecker, like the Mojo Woodpecker, has terrific coloring. It's predominantly black with some white, red and yellow markings. Instead of using a rotating wing system like the Mojo it uses an "up and down" flapping wing. Like the Mojo, it can be run with both wings moving or just one. Of the two, I feel the Edge unit is a bit more realistic with regard to imitating a flapping wounded bird. This unit is designed to be clipped to a branch or fence (due to the nature of the clip, it will only hang upside down when used on a fence, which I do not believe hurts the presentation) or suspended from the loop on the back. The only down side to this unit is that the motor noise is a bit loud, but by the time a predator gets close enough to hear it, it should be too late.

Decoy Heart Predator Supreme

When introduced nearly 10 years ago, this was one of the first decoys to break from the traditional idea that a decoy had to look exactly like a rabbit to be successful. George Brint, the designer/inventor, broke from the norm and used a stylistic jack-tail-groundhog (my term) design that really looks like nothing and everything at the same time. Slipped over the ball shaped Decoy Heart, which is mounted on a wooden dowel by means of a spring, this unit paved they way for further "outside the box" decoy designs. I started using this decoy years ago and had great results. Occasionally tough to insert into rough ground, the wooden decoy stake could be improved upon with a sharper, tougher steel unit, but other than that this decoy is as effective as it is simple.

The granite-look *rock base of the Edge All Call works well when rocky or frozen ground is an issue.*

Edge All Call

This unit would make a great western decoy where the ground is so rocky and/or frozen that inserting any type of stake is nearly impossible. The Edge All Call overcomes this obstacle by utilizing its own granite-look rock base with an adjustable-for-height rod and decoy affixed on top.

This decoy has several unique features. It is designed to react and move in time with calling, and has a sensitivity adjustment knob to fine tune the unit. It also has a built in amplifier that can increase the output of electronic calls that are plugged into the unit.

My only complaint with the unit is the decoy is a bit small for long range acquisition. A multi-head version with different furry critters would go a long way towards making this decoy ideal for many applications.

Come Alive Predator Enticer

This unit is interesting for several reasons, beginning with the design of the decoy. As we are seeing from more scientific studies done in relation to predator vision, mimicking nature is probably not the best option when creating a decoy. The Come Alive decoy capitalizes on that and comes from the factory with two colors of heads that are easily interchangeable. The first one is predominantly black with some white and red markings while the other one is white with some red markings. Comprised of soft marabou-type feathers mounted on an ultra-flexible spring, even with the unit turned off it looks like it is moving. These heads would also be easy to make yourself with cheap materials from the fly-tying store. You could make practically any color combination.

The height of the unit is controlled by several segments of fiberglass rod put together with rubber slip joints. The electronic box and battery holder sits on the ground so the overall height is adjustable by simply using more or fewer rods. It is designed to work as an intermittent decoy and was one of the most realistic intermittent decoys I tested. The on/off ratio can be customized inside the unit. While an overall interesting design, it could be improved upon with a stiffer rod system

DECOY COLOR

Predators see colors differently than humans. For this reason, don't be afraid to customize your decoy with home-made material to affect the color and presentation. Some ideas are strips of colored cloth, dyed marabou feathers or rabbit fur srips (both available at fly tying shops) glued onto the main decoy. Some hunters have even used spray paint or fabric dye to change the color of the body of their decoy.

Cats are especially susceptible to decoys. They come in slow and cautious, looking for anything suspicious, and a moving decoy will generally fix their attention.

in a more muted color than white. While it would work well in the snow or in soft Midwest farm fields, this unit would be tough to get to stand up in many places across the West where rocky, sandy or frozen soil reign supreme.

Sniper Predator Styx Feather Dancer

This decoy reminds me very much of my first attempt at creating a decoy with a rabbit skin on a stick. While the principle is the same as that first decoy, this unit is much better than my early attempts. Essentially the Feather Dancer is a jointed, camo-dipped aluminum shaft that can be disassembled for easy transport. The bottom is sharply pointed to aid penetration into hard ground. The top is affixed with a swiveling devise that allows for unencumbered 360-degree movement. From the swivel is a string attached to one large boldly marked turkey feather. That's it. No batteries, no intermittent intervals, no sound amplifier. Just a turkey tail on a stick. But boy how effective it is! As far as sight goes, the colors are right for predators and the movement created by even the faintest touch of Mother Nature's breath imparts movement that rivals any battery powered decoy. Simple, lightweight, easy to carry, effective....that's the name of the game in my book.

Especially in *the open country of the West, decoys can make a difference, as the Author's brother, Greg, discovered.*

CHAPTER 4

COYOTE CALLS
OLD AND NEW

There is no doubt about it, calls are an essential part
of this sport and in my opinion are what makes it
so alluring. Don't get me wrong, shooting a predator by happenstance, by spotting and stalking or
by driving is still fun, but there is something to be
said for communicating with a predator and convincing it to come
to you. Luckily for predator hunters who love calls, each year has
gotten better than the last with more and more innovations hitting
the fields every day.

This is a good thing; more choices ultimately lead to a superior
product at a lower price. But with all this diversification and compe-
tition, how does one choose which call is right for them?

What are the differences between wood and plastic, open reed
and closed reed, close range calls and long range calls? By understanding these differences you will be able to make an educated
choice and get the right call to fit your style, region and/or hunting
conditions.

Calls are really pretty simple with two primary variables: reed
type and body material. All other features (tone, purpose, cost, etc.)
are influenced by these two factors. To pick the right call for you,
start by examining the influences of these two factors.

Reed Types
The difference between open and closed reed calls has to do with
the reed type in the call body.

A closed reed call typically features a small reed, usually made from metal (but can be plastic or Mylar) that is fixed within the barrel of the call. This type of reed produces a "pre-set" sound when air passes through it.

An open reed call generally sports a much larger reed which is exposed from the call body itself. This type of call requires not only that air pass through it, but that pressure (either from the lips or teeth) be applied to produce the tone and pitch desired.

These two types of reeds are used in 90% of the calls today. There are also diaphragm-type calls (commonly used in the turkey and elk calling world) and split reed-type predator calls, characterized by a reed sandwiched by a flexible mouthpiece.

There are pros and cons for each design. According to Mark Zepp, noted coyote video producer and call manufacturer, "The benefits to a closed reed call are simple – they are easy to operate, they produce very realistic prey-in-distress sounds with very little practice, and are often economical. The downside is they can freeze up in low temperatures rendering them useless, and they are limited in the sounds they are capable of making."

> Luckily for predator hunters who love calls, each year has gotten better than the last with more and more innovations hitting the fields every day.

Open reed calls shine where closed reeds fail, but do come with their own set of limitations. Zepp continues, "Open reed calls are great because one call can do everything from a rodent squeak, to a whipped pup, to a mature coyote howl and virtually every sound in between. They don't usually freeze up in cold weather, but an open reed call can cost a bit more and will take more practice to learn how to use effectively."

So what type of call should you get? The good news is that you can have more than one. The bad news is that calls can become an addiction. Don't say you weren't warned. I have many different calls and choosing the select few to carry into the field can be a chore in itself. Generally I carry at least one closed reed and an open reed for no other reason than sometimes a particular coyote just likes the way one sounds. Plus, if one freezes up I have a backup.

Body Materials

Traditionally predator calls were made from wood. As manufacturing techniques and new materials evolved after WWII, more and more calls were manufactured from plastic, aluminum and various synthetic materials. Today hunters can choose from a wide variety of materials including wood, injection molded plastic, machined (turned) polymer and metal. Like individual design and reed type, the choice in materials affects the performance and overall sound. While all materials have certain attributes and characteristics, possibly the biggest factor to consider when choosing a body material is plain old tonal quality to your ear. Every hunter has a different calling style and prefers particular sound characteristics. Choose a call you like to blow, have confidence in it and you will have success.

Wood

Not only does wood look good to the eye and feel nice in the hand, it also resonates sound well. While a coyote call is not as precise as a Gibson guitar, the idea remains the same – quality sound comes from quality wood. The downsides of wood are relatively few, but it should be noted that they can cost slightly more than synthetic calls because they are handmade, raw materials cost a bit more and the finish work takes more time. That being said, the

A BETTER LANYARD

If you are tired of traditional call lanyards banging calls together, making noise and getting tangled up, try this method. Anglers often use small coil retractors or "zippers" to attach various fly accouterments to their vest for easy access. Select a couple of the larger models and affix your mouth calls to them with a small eye ring attached around the body of the call with a zip tie. Attach the "zippers" to various places on your hunting coat or vest and you have all your calls instantly accessible, as well as separated. When not in use, they automatically retract back to the vest where they remain noise free.

Mouth calls *come in open and closed-reed styles and in many materials and configurations, including plastic, metal, polymer, natural horn and wood.*

cost increase is pretty modest and, depending upon manufacturer, sometimes non-existent.

Another potential downside is that, depending upon the quality of the finish, a wood call may be affected by external humidity or moisture. When humidity is high or if the call has absorbed moisture (from being inside your clothing as you sweat your way up a hill) sometimes it can swell then shrink, making closed reed assemblies tough to keep in place. Depending on moisture content, the sound produced by a wood call may also vary considerably.

Molded Plastic

Many calls today are made from injection molded plastic. Injected bodies are cheap to produce, require little manual labor to manufacture, remain relatively unaffected by external conditions and sound pretty darn good.

The downside to injection molded plastic can be the depth or resonance of the sound produced. Keep in mind however that the quality of sound produced from a molded plastic call varies widely from manufacturer to manufacturer. Some calls are thin, cheap plastic affairs that do not perform well, while others are extremely close to a custom call in terms of sound and quality. You truly get what you pay for in injection molded calls.

Acrylic Polymer

Acrylic polymer is a high-density plastic that is often turned on a lathe, much like wood, to produce extremely loud, long range calls with a deep resonating timbre. While this material dominates the competitive waterfowling market, it has made few inroads into the predator calling scene, mainly due to its expensive nature. However, a few custom call manufacturers are utilizing it with very good results. If you are willing to spend the money, this material produces one of the finest, non-varying sounds available.

> The sounds produced by a metal call are unique, often high pitched, and carry well over long distance.

Metal

Over the years several manufacturers have tried using various metals as a call body with mixed results. The sounds produced by a metal call are unique, often high pitched, and carry well over long distance. But what many call manufacturers didn't consider is metal gets very cold and when left in its original state is shiny and reflective, alerting wary predators. However, the main manufacturers utilizing metal today understand these issues and coat their calls with camouflage dip-type finishes that solve both problems. In addition to covering the metal, many manufacturers using metal are also using open reed designs with a plastic mouthpiece, thereby eliminating the "cold" factor.

Brand Review

Zepp

Zepp calls, long known in coon hunting circles, have exploded into the predator market in recent years. Combining years of in-the-field product development with the latest manufacturing techniques and designs, Zepp calls are not only unique in design and material, but are extremely effective on predators. I have used Zepp's entire lineup with success, but my two favorite have to be the Rattler and the 1080.

The Rattler is a double dual closed reed call (four reeds in all), which sports a powder-coated metal body. This call is extremely compact but packs a mighty punch. Few calls are this raspy and loud, which makes for a perfect windy-day closed reed call.

The plastic bodied, open reed 1080 (named after the predator control poison) is as versatile as the Rattler is loud. Like its name suggests, it truly is poison on predators. For 2008 Zepp introduced a unique crow and coyote combination, which from initial reports and field tests will live up to Zepp's reputation of making calls that kill predators.

Burnham Brothers

I have a soft spot for Burnham Brothers game calls, as the first call I ever plunked down my hard-earned lawn mowing money for was a Burnham S-2 (from Murray Burnham himself at a sport show nearly 20 years ago). It is one call I still have in my collection and it has accounted for its fair share of predators. While technically it is an open reed call, it is unique with a split body style. Simply insert it into your mouth like a harmonica and you can call hands free when the shot comes or cup your hands around your mouth to direct and

...the first call I ever plunked down my hard-earned lawn mowing money for was a Burnham S-2.

amplify the sound. Other great calls in the Burnham lineup include the Black Magic, the Deluxe Predator, the Long Range and the Mini Blaster. I have personally used all of these calls with great results and many predators have fallen to them all over the U.S.

Predator Sniper Calls (Tri State Outdoors)

Well-known for their innovative, high-quality shooting sticks, Predator Sniper Styx recently released three new calls that re-

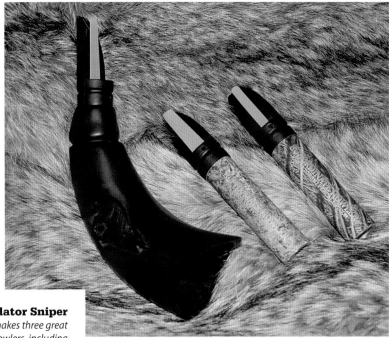

Predator Sniper
makes three great howlers, including an injection-molded cow horn and two aluminum-bodied, open reed howlers.

flect the same innovative mentality. Concentrating on coyote vocalization, all of their calls are large, open reed howlers. The first two (the Alpha Male and the Subordinate Howler) combine modern manufacturing techniques and materials, such as dipped camo covered aluminum and plastic mouth pieces, while the third (Buffalo Horn Howler) is a synthetic but faithful reproduction of an authentic buffalo horn howler. The sound quality from these calls is extremely good and all have the ability to perfectly recreate the sounds of coyote vocalization as well as carry across large, windy landscapes.

Circe/Lohman

Circe/Lohman has a long history of making wood closed reed calls, but they also make a great line of open reed calls. Their Open Season Predator creates a wide range of prey-in-distress sounds as well as realistic coyote barks and yips. Their Ki-Yoter features a wider bell-shaped body and a large reed allowing for a high volume of air passing through for loud sounds and realistic coyote vocalization.

Moving to their closed reed line, one of my favorites is their Professional 3 Calls-In-One model. While it is kind of gimmicky, it does work well. Utilizing three different pitched, closed reeds inside the plastic body, all it takes is a simple twist of the mouthpiece to select realistic jack rabbit, cottontail and coaxer calls.

Johnny Stewart

Johnny Stewart, along with Murry Burnham, is known in the world of calling as one of the founding fathers of the sport. While the Johnny Stewart company was better known for electronic calls, they were never a slouch on the lung-powered variety either. I particularly like their Crit'r Getter Mini. This compact call not only sounds great, but is loud as well. It is an excellent open reed call that can be slipped into the pocket. In addition to their time-proven calls, Johnny Stewart has recently released the Mac Daddy Coaxer and the Mac Daddy Howler. Both are variable pitched calls capable of making a wide range of sounds.

> Johnny Stewart, along with Murry Burnham, is known in the world of calling as one of the founding fathers of the sport.

Crit'R Call

Crit'R Call can be characterized as practical, inexpensive, and easy to use. In both the Standard and Magnum offering, it produces a wide range of sounds, including rodent-in-distress and standard prey-in-distress, and does a very passable coyote howl. What I like most about this call is the versatility and interchangeability of parts. The Standard comes packaged with an extra .014 thick reed, reed block and reed band, while the Magnum comes with a .010 reed and a .0085 reed, extra reed blocks and band. The one complaint I have with both of these models is the lack of a lanyard notch, which makes them difficult to keep at hand in the field. Over the years, I have lost enough of these calls across the West to outfit a small predator hunting club.

Dan Thompson Calls

World Champion caller Dan Thompson of Rawlins, Wyoming, is considered by many to be the modern dean of calling. He has probably forgotten more about coyote calling than most of us will ever learn. Thompson manufactures several types and styles of calls, but probably his three best known are his Weems replica (designed after the famous Weems closed reed call of the 1950's); his Red Desert howler, a very loud open reed call; and his PC-1 closed reed call. When asked what makes his calls so successful, Thompson said, "I strive for quality from the first step to the final delivered product. If it is going to carry my name, it has to perform well."

Dan Thompson
makes awesome closed and open reed calls.

Primos

Primos, known for one of the largest call lines of any manufacturer, has an extensive range of high-quality predator calls, including a unique line of Randy Anderson Signature calls. At last count Primos was making over a dozen various open and closed reed predator calls.

Some of my favorites in each category include the Double Wammy, a unique dual open reed design; the Still Cottontail Rabbit closed reed calls; and the Mini-Mag open reed howler. With so many choices, how does a person know which one to buy? According to TJ Williams, Vice President of Sales and Marketing for Primos, "Our most successful calls have to be the Little Dog and the Hot Dog because they really do everything – from prey-in-distress to coyote vocalization. This is one call that does it all."

> At last count Primos was making over a dozen various open and closed reed predator calls.

Sceery

Sceery has a wide range of game calls including several models of predator calls. Notable is their distinctive camo rubber coating, which is quiet when calls inadvertently bang against a gun stock or other calls. While I own several Sceery calls, ranging from older, wood varmint-getters to modern open reed marvels, my favorite Sceery call has to be the Double Barreled High Pitched Predator Call. With its unique double open reed and barrel design, this call provides a wide range of sounds, making it suitable for a wide array of predators.

STEALTHY APPROACH

Mounting a squeaker bulb on your forearm is a great way to keep a short-range, freeze-proof call handy. However, they are easily bumped while getting in and out of a vehicle or while trying to walk quietly to a stand. Eliminate this unwanted noise by adding a large rubber band around the call, effectively displacing all the air. Once on stand, roll the rubber band down the forearm and you have a fully functional call again. When ready to move, put the rubber band back on and you can go in silence.

Custom/Semi-Custom Calls

While the world of predator call-ing has always been well represented by custom call manufacturers, it seems that today there are more then ever before. Whether you are looking for fancy wood, high-end polymer or metal, in an open or closed reed design, there is a custom call manufacturer out there to fit the bill.

Some of my favorites include Long Valley Predator Calls, Arizona Game Calls, Hogsback Custom acrylic and Dogwood Creek Custom Calls. All are excellent examples of the custom call maker's art.

> Whether you are looking for fancy wood, high-end polymer or metal, in an open or closed reed design, there is a custom call manufacturer out there to fit the bill.

Bulbs and Squeakers

Bulbs (or Squeakers, as they are sometimes called) also play a vital role in a predator hunter's arsenal. Their big advantages are that they are almost com-pletely movement-free to use, can be se-cured to the forearm of a gun for use on the final approach and generally don't freeze up in cold weather since there is no moisture passing through the reed.

While not an all-around call, they should not be left at home either as they have their place in the right circumstances.

Electronic Calls

Since I first started predator hunting, electronic calls have literally changed the sport. In my early years, I still recall using a primitive electronic call that actually took micro-sized mini records. When I graduated to a tape playing model with an external

The Phantom Pro-Series *call can be purchased as a wired unit or as a wireless remote system.*

55

speaker I was ecstatic (even though the heavy battery pack made it quite a load to carry).

Today the electronic revolution has gone completely digital and is offered in many configurations that sound better, are lighter and easier to use than ever before.

This late winter **coyote** *fell for a remotely-placed FOXPRO rabbit-in-distress sound. Note the squeaker bulb mounted on forend of the rifle. These calls work well to close the final distance with a predator, and they have the unique advantage of rarely freezing up.*

Brand Review

FOXPRO

When it comes to calls, there is little argument that FOXPRO is one of the giants on the electronics side of the business. This is for good reason. They manufacture extremely durable, solid-state digital calls that not only hold up in the field but also sound fantastic. With too many electronic models to cover in one chapter, I have included a couple of their newer calls.

One of their newest calls is the Fury. With 2GB of internal storage space, the Fury is a tank! It can hold up to 500 sounds. It comes pre-loaded with a 100 sounds from FOXPRO's library, and can play MP3s, uncompressed WAV, and FXP (FOXPRO's proprietary file type).

To keep the sounds loud and realistic, the Fury has dual speakers. The individually amplified horn (front) and cone (rear) speaker combination provides loud, crystal-clear audio and great frequency response. In addition to the two internal speakers, hunters can add up to two external speakers. All speakers can be controlled from the TX-500 remote control.

Using a remote control gives the hunter a lot of flexibility and FOXPRO's new TX-500 allows even more freedom. By utilizing FHSS technology, remote range and reliability at longer distances has greatly increased over previous models. In addition to range, another significant improvement

> When it comes to calls, there is little argument that FOXPRO is one of the giants on the electronics side of the business

over previous remotes is the extra large, backlit LCD navigation menu, which you can scroll through or directly enter sounds.

Another great FOXPRO call – one I have been using for several years now – is the FX5. While not as advanced as the Fury, it still gets the job done for me day in and day out. It stores and plays up to 200 sounds in 1 GB of memory, with four custom presets for your favorite sounds and volume levels. The FX5 comes from the factory with 50 preloaded sounds of your choice (it will play MP3, uncompressed WAV, and FXP files).

The sound quality is also impressive with two internal speakers, each with its own amplifier for improved frequency

FOXPRO calls
*combine incredible
digital sound with
durability and
functionality.*

response and increased volume, and one speaker jack for an external speaker. You can select one, two or three speakers to play at the same time.

As high tech as FOXPRO's electronic calls are, the big news is that they have also entered the world of mouth calls with a pretty unique open reed design called the Skyote. The first thing I noticed about the Skyote was the raised tone board with a ridge around it. The concept behind this ridge is to prevent the reed from freezing to the tone board in cold weather. Since I often have calls freeze up, this feature obviously caught my attention. In addition to the Skyote, they also introduced a tiny key chain with a closed reed call inserted into it. While it may not be my first choice as a primary call, it is nice to know you always have a call along on any trip, even if just to annoy the other folks in the car.

With the Power Dogg *from Primos, there are no sound cards, cassettes, speakers or wires to fuss with. The unit is extremely weather resistant and durable.*

Primos

The Primos Power Dogg is a water resistant, durable electronic unit with a neoprene gasket sealed housing. Tipping the scales at 1.8 pounds, the Power Dogg operates in temperatures down to -4° F. The unit has 12 sounds to choose from including coyote vocalization, prey-in-distress, crow and snow goose. All predator sounds are made by Randy Anderson while the other sounds are made by the Primos team. The remote for the unit has a large LCD display and works from over 100 yards away. While not as advanced as some of the other electronic calls on the market, it is a quality unit that is a fair buy for the price.

Johnny Stewart

The new Johnny Stewart PM-4 Wireless Preymaster Caller incorporates all of the features of the original Preymaster Caller with some added extras. The PM-4 features a wireless remote with a range of 100 yards (up to 250 yards in optimal conditions). The handheld remote transmitter has a water-resistant keypad with raised buttons for each sound, making it easy to operate with gloves or at night. The base unit has three slots that are compatible with all available Preymaster memory cards for up to 12 available sounds.

Burnham Brothers

Burnham Brothers has been designing and manufacturing electronic predator calls for over 55 years. Using actual recordings of animals, Burnham Brothers electronic calls sound super realistic. Their Compucaller comes in a Mossy Oak camo water-resistant carrying bag and includes a built in amplifier and a 20 watt speaker. The remote features a backlit LCD screen that displays signal strength, battery levels, current sound playing and volume level.

The Compucaller comes with 16 sounds, including grown cottontail, cottontail duet, baby cottontail, half-grown jackrabbit, yellowhammer woodpecker, coyote pup and cottontail, coyote howl, lip squeak, grown jackrabbit, fawn in distress, canine pup, coyote pup whining, grey fox pup, baby raccoon, pair of crows and crows fighting over baby crow.

Compucaller III digital game caller comes with a long range, two-way remote control and 16 high-quality predator calling sounds (with the ability to hold 32).

CHAPTER

5

CHALLENGING HUNTING ENVIRONMENTS

I f predator hunters have their own heaven, it will probably be miles and miles of sage flats with enough undulations and rises to provide ample elevation for making stands. The wind will never blow and the temperature will always be in the low 20s. For now, that's not the reality we live in. Predators are found from coast to coast in a variety of habitat, weather seldom cooperates and sometimes interesting natural formations get in the way of success. But until we all get a chance to hunt the happy hunting grounds, these challenges will have to be faced. Here are a few situations I call *challenging hunting environments* and how to deal with them.

Calling in the Wind

Late one night in a rustic cabin in South Dakota, the sound of the single pane windows doing their best to pop out of their frames woke me from a sound slumber. It was doubtful the gale would blow itself out before the alarm went off in two hours. I dozed back to sleep and hoped for the best. When the alarm went off I didn't need to look outside at the flag pole to know that hunting would be miserable. The temperature was in the low 30s and, from the sounds of the metal roof threatening to tear loose, I knew the wind had not died down. If this was home, I would have gone back to sleep. Since my partner and I drove the better part of six hours to get to this "coyote mecca," I rolled out from under the warm covers and started some coffee.

When hunting
blustery open country, sometimes deep canyons will remain out of the wind, providing micro calling areas that will produce all day.

I have lived and hunted in some windy places over the years, places where the scrubby pinions and junipers grow at a 45-degree angle with the wind. Some of the more notable wind tunnels include Wyoming's high desert, as well as the plains of Nebraska, North Dakota and South Dakota. I am here to tell you that, if you have a choice, you are far better off simply not hunting than trying to call in a coyote when the wind is blowing more than 20 miles an hour.

In the wind, your calling is severely limited in every direction with the exception of straight downwind. As any predator hunter who has been busted by a coyote can tell you, while down-wind calling is not completely worthless, it is right in the same neck of the woods! Aside from the fact that predators have limited hearing range, for the most part they are doing what you should be doing: staying out of the wind and resting. They are not out cruising around, which further reduces your opportunities. Finally, it is just plain miserable to be there most of the time. Sticking it out and making a stand or walking over the next rise to set up again becomes a chore in itself. Windy calling is surely for the purist (or masochist) who really wants to stack the odds in the predator's favor.

> Windy calling is for the purist (or masochist) who really wants to stack the odds in the predator's favor.

All that being said, if you drove all night to get to a spot, are in a tournament or simply have to get out from under foot at home, then there are a few things that can slightly tip the odds back in your favor and help salvage an otherwise scrapped day.

Windy Day Techniques

Calling in the wind doesn't completely change calling strategy, but it does force you to refine it. One of the biggest changes is in how far you'll move after calling before making another stand. On a calm day, after I call at a stand I generally walk back to the pickup and head a couple of miles to a new destination. Not so on a windy day. On a calm day it is generally true that a mouth call can be heard at least a mile by a coyote. Depending on the intensity of the wind, this distance is easily cut in half. I have hunted days where 300 yards was probably the maximum distance a call could be heard.

Using remote electronic callers *and positioning on the lee side of a hill can help increase your range on windy days.*

It's easy to see that standard calling techniques are not going to be as effective with this loss of coverage. For this reason, after making a stand I generally don't drive away in search of another prime spot; I relocate a couple hundred yards and call again. In canyon and ridge-type country, several stands can be made all within a several hundred yard area, calling in different directions and into the various canyons. Keep in mind, regardless of how far a predator can hear, every 200 yards you walk is an additional 200 yards of new territory you are covering with a call. By slowly moving through an area and being stealthy, you can effectively cover all the country regardless of how windy it is.

When the wind howls *across open country, look for natural features that help block the wind. In this case a deep cut provided enough protection to hold dogs. With loud calling, we finally enticed one out of this cut where he was bedded.*

In addition to making multiple stands, I look for a different type of country than on calm days. When the weather is calm most coyotes are out and about looking for a meal. If they are not out they are just as likely to be bedded up under a sage bush as they are in a deep canyon cut. When the wind howls this all changes. When it is really blowing, most predators are hunkered down, out of the wind, in brushy draws, tree patches or broken country that buffers them from the brunt of the wind. The few that are still out looking for a meal are generally close to these natural protective features. By sneaking in close to these resting areas and calling, you stand a much better chance than hitting your traditional spots.

Before calling, get ready for an immediate shot. On windy days, stealthy hunters can get extremely close to predators without being detected. More than once I have had a coyote jump out of a patch of thick brush within rock throwing distance from my calling position. They generally stare for a brief moment before running off. The ready rifleman will put fur on the ground; the unprepared one will go home empty handed. Before calling, get your rifle pointed at the most likely direction (you can rest assured a coyote will come from anywhere but here), turn the scope down to its lowest power setting, and be ready to shoot within seconds of blowing the call.

> On windy days, stealthy hunters can get extremely close to predators without being detected.

Case in point: This past season my brother, a friend and I were calling in another notoriously windy part of the country, the Lemhi Valley in Idaho. This country is so big you spend your first few days just walking around staring in awe at the far mountains and the miles and miles of sage brush in between. As the air comes off those mountains and down through the valleys it can pick up quite a head of steam. The day in question was one of those days that we would have been better off sitting in a local watering hole watching the football game, but I was due to catch a flight out the following morning so we were making the most of the bad opportunity.

The wind was a constant 30-plus miles an hour howl from the east and the temperature was hovering in the high 20s. We knew no coyote would be out hunting those big open flats in conditions like this, so we started looking for deep cuts in the basalt rock, looking for a lee side that would provide protection for a bedded coyote. After looking around for awhile we found an ideal spot to set up and start calling.

Our hunting buddy Taro set up behind us 30 yards and started calling with his FOXPRO. Even at full volume, it was barely audible from our position, but it wasn't 30 seconds and my brother hissed, "There's a coyote right in front of us!" I looked 100 yards or so out on the flat while fiddling with the record button on my camera when I caught movement right in front of us – and by right in front of us, I mean within two steps! The coyote must have been bedded right at the base of the rock formation we choose to set up on and he was in the process of climbing up the car-sized rock we were sitting on.

Before I could turn on the camera he saw us, turned and bolted. He beelined it straight away but wasn't running full tilt – still a do-able shot. However, my brother had the scope turned up and the rifle resting on shooting sticks, so by the time he got them off the sticks and found the coyote in the sage the dog was home free. It just goes to show that when calling in windy conditions you are far more likely than not to be blanked on a set up, but when you do succeed there is a good chance it will be up close and personal. Keep the rifle ready or, better yet, leave the rifle on the bipod and cradle a shotgun in your lap. When the wind howls you may find ample opportunity to use it.

Modify Your Calling Frequency

On windy days I call much more frequently than I do on calm days. If you have ever sat apart from your calling partner when the wind is gusting, you will agree you only hear about every third call. If the caller happens to be blowing when there is a lull between gusts, the call can be heard. If he is calling during the middle of a gust, chances are it won't. For this reason I call more frequently on stand when the wind is blowing. However, I don't call for as long a duration as I would on a calm day.

> On windy days I call much more frequently than I do on calm days ... However, I don't call for as long a duration as I would on a calm day.

In my experience, on a calm day coyotes can hear the call over a mile away and will respond from that distance if they are hungry. That is generally why I stay on stand 15 or so minutes: Ninety percent of those that will come can travel that distance within this time frame. The same holds true for windy days. It is just that the distance is much less. I plan for about seven minutes per stand after the first call is made when the wind is howling. In five minutes any hungry coyotes in a 600-yard radius can make it in or show their presence if they are coming slowly. If they don't show during that time, odds are they are not going to budge (or there aren't any) no matter how much you call. While I only stick around for seven minutes, it doesn't mean the hunt is over. I quickly sneak to another position 50 or 100 yards away facing a different direction and repeat the stand.

The key is to *sneak* to the next spot. Don't silhouette yourself, don't take undue time packing up equipment, collapsing bipods etc. Utilize cover and natural depressions. Occasionally when you move you will spot a slow-moving coyote on his way in, and as long as you spot him before he spots you the game is still on.

Choosing the Right Call

Picking the right areas and calling them thoroughly is important on windy days. Picking the right call is equally important. Once again, the whole point on a windy day is to be heard as far as possible. That's why you get close and call often. You also must choose a call with the range to really reach out to coyotes.

On calm days I have had coyotes a few hundred yards away hear quiet rodent squeaks I made with my mouth on the palm of my hand. On stormy days I have blown for all I was worth on a normal rabbit call and had coyotes (that were not much further away) never turn their heads. In these situations you need a call that will carry. For maximum volume I prefer calls with bodies made from acrylic or aluminum, with multiple closed reeds or large open reeds. In addition to loud standard-sized

For maximum volume I prefer calls with bodies made from acrylic or aluminum, with multiple closed reeds or large open reeds.

calls, I have also successfully used large open reed howlers blown like a jackrabbit-in-distress call. One thing is for sure: All of these calls will take a lot of lung power to really get the sound out of them, but they will reward hunters with results.

I also like high-quality electronic calls, as they can produce some loud noise. Keep in mind not all electronic calls are loud, but digital units with high-quality large speakers or, better yet, external amplified speakers, designed for long range work, can nicely cut through a howling wind.

Choosing a Wind Gun

The upside to hunting in the wind is it gives hunters an excuse to buy another predator rifle. If you've ever tried explaining the need for so many different rifles to a spouse you can appreciate this reasoning. Just like summer and winter clothes, there are windy day rifles and calm day rifles. If the weather is calm, I generally hunt with some variety of .22 centerfire or my beloved .17 Remington. But when the wind picks up past 15 mph, I grab a gun better suited to the task.

Just like summer and winter clothes, there are windy day rifles and calm day rifles.

The biggest problem rifles face in the wind is bullet drift. This can be reduced (but not eliminated) by larger diameter, heavier bullets (design of the bullet also plays a part, but the most significant factor is weight). For windy day rifles, I start with .243 and go up to about .270 caliber. You can go bigger but it is generally not necessary. In addition to larger-than-normal calibers, I like low-powered variable scopes, since many times you are calling in close quarters or trying to pick up a running target.

The spouse may counter your need for a new rifle by pointing out that if you are hunting such tight quarters wind drift shouldn't be much of a problem – and he/she is correct. However, remind your beloved that even though most shots are close, sometimes they are far and the difference between a .17 Remington and a .25-06 at 300 yards is about a yard stick in length. This makes hitting a predator on the hoof a difficult proposition. Finally, remind them that the price of having the right tool for the job will be easily paid for with

All guns *are not created equal. When the wind starts to howl, look for a rifle that is chambered in a large enough caliber to minimize bullet drift.*

all the pelts you harvest. (Okay, that argument didn't work so well for me either.)

While it is important to have a rifle that can buck the wind in a long shot situation, you also stand a good chance of getting a predator up close and personal. For this kind of shooting I prefer a shotgun. Pick a quality pump or autoloader. I like to equip mine with TRU GLO Ghost ring sights, but any fiber optic bead or sight system will also work. Screw in a full or extra full choke (maybe even open it up a bit in really thick cover), load it with BBs or Ts and you're in business.

Hunting Out of the Box

This next section may or may not be met with much approval from calling purists, but the methods described are extremely effective. For those more interested with the end results than the means to an end, these methods are worth a try.

Walking Draws

As stated earlier, coyotes will often hole up on windy days, riding out the storm. One of their favorite places to hide out in the open plains is in a tight, brush-choked draw sheltered from the wind. These are often the spots I look for to call from, but they also make excellent choices for the walking hunter. While calling is effective in these tight areas, sometimes there is no good approach to make a stand or the wind is blowing too hard to be heard even up close. In these situations, try hunting song dogs like you would pheasants. Two hunters can generally cover a single draw effectively. Start at the widest point and walk towards the end. Like pheasant hunting, the objective is to flush them from the thick cover. If the draw is clad in medium to sparse vegetation, walking along the outside will generally flush all of the coyotes in the area. If it is brush choked, filled with tumble weeds or has steep sides, sometimes one of the

> Sometimes there is no good approach to make a stand or the wind is blowing too hard to be heard even up close. In these situations, try hunting song dogs like you would pheasants.

hunters will need to get right in the middle of it while keeping the other hunter on the outside walking parallel to the "beater."

Don't expect pretty, standing broadside shots in either scenario. When coyotes flush from a draw, they often come fast with their tail tucked and a full head of steam. A two-gun approach (one hunter with a rifle, the other with a shotgun loaded with BBs or larger) is often the best strategy.

When walking a draw, another good technique is to use one hunter as a blocker at a natural funnel or escape route. More times than I can count I've had coyotes and bobcats sneak away from the walking hunter right into the lap of the blocker.

Spot and Stalk

While not a classic calling approach, one of my favorite techniques on windy days in open country is spot and stalk. Where coyotes have cover they will use it and most of the time become invisible from a distance. In sparse, open country, "heavy" cover often means the lee side of open hills, blown out cut banks, hay bales and small clumps of sage or yucca bushes.

Wait until mid-morning, then ascend the tallest point around with a high-powered spotting scope. By this time in the morning almost all coyotes have laid up for the day. By sitting and examining every likely out-of-the-wind hiding spot, you can often spot them curled up in a ball with their nose tucked under their tail. After spotting one, stalk it like you would stalk any other species. Use ground cover, low spots and ridgebacks to get within range. While trying to put the sneak on a coyote on a calm day is very difficult, the howling wind covers most sounds and makes predicting the path of your scent very easy. With a little practice, you can set up your bipod within easy shooting range of a still slumbering coyote.

> While trying to put the sneak on a coyote on a calm day is very difficult, the howling wind covers most sounds and makes predicting the path of your scent very easy.

As you can see there are many ways to skin a cat, or in this case call a coyote. When the wind blows and you have to hunt, don't give up. Grab a rifle, a loud call, some new tricks and head for the field. By working with the wind instead of against it, the results may just surprise you.

Hunting the Mountains

Hunting in the mountains presents another challenging environment, but it can be extremely productive.

Many hunters think of coyote and predator hunting in general as a Great Plains sport. From Texas to Canada, if there are rolling wheat fields, basalt rock bluffs or sage brush, a hunter's mind instinctively turns to predator hunting. I know I've been guilty of this mentality from time to time, and with good reason. A whole host of predators, including coyotes, bobcats and fox, thrive in these open, semi-arid places. Not only do they thrive, they are easy to see in open country, perhaps making

> Hunting in the mountains presents another challenging environment, but it can be extremely productive.

them appear more numerous than they actually are. Finally, calling predators in open flat country is generally highly productive; the sound carries well when there are no mountains, trees and roaring rivers to block its path.

So that leads us to the question, "If a call is blown in mountainous country and a predator isn't there to hear it, does it still make a sound?"

While my college philosophy professor would probably still give me an "F" if he could, the good news for hunters is that the question is rarely relevant, as there are lots of predators waiting to come to the call in mountainous country. Even better is the vast amount of land, much of which is public, that is considered mountainous.

The entire west coast from the Pacific to the eastern slopes of the Rocky Mountains, from the Arctic to nearly southern California, is one continuous mountain range. Eastern hunters can get in on mountain hunting as well in the Smoky and Appalachian Mountains. Not to be left out, the heartland of America is home to the large Ozark range with its expansive Mark Twain National Forest tucked in its center. In all, no less than 25 states can be considered

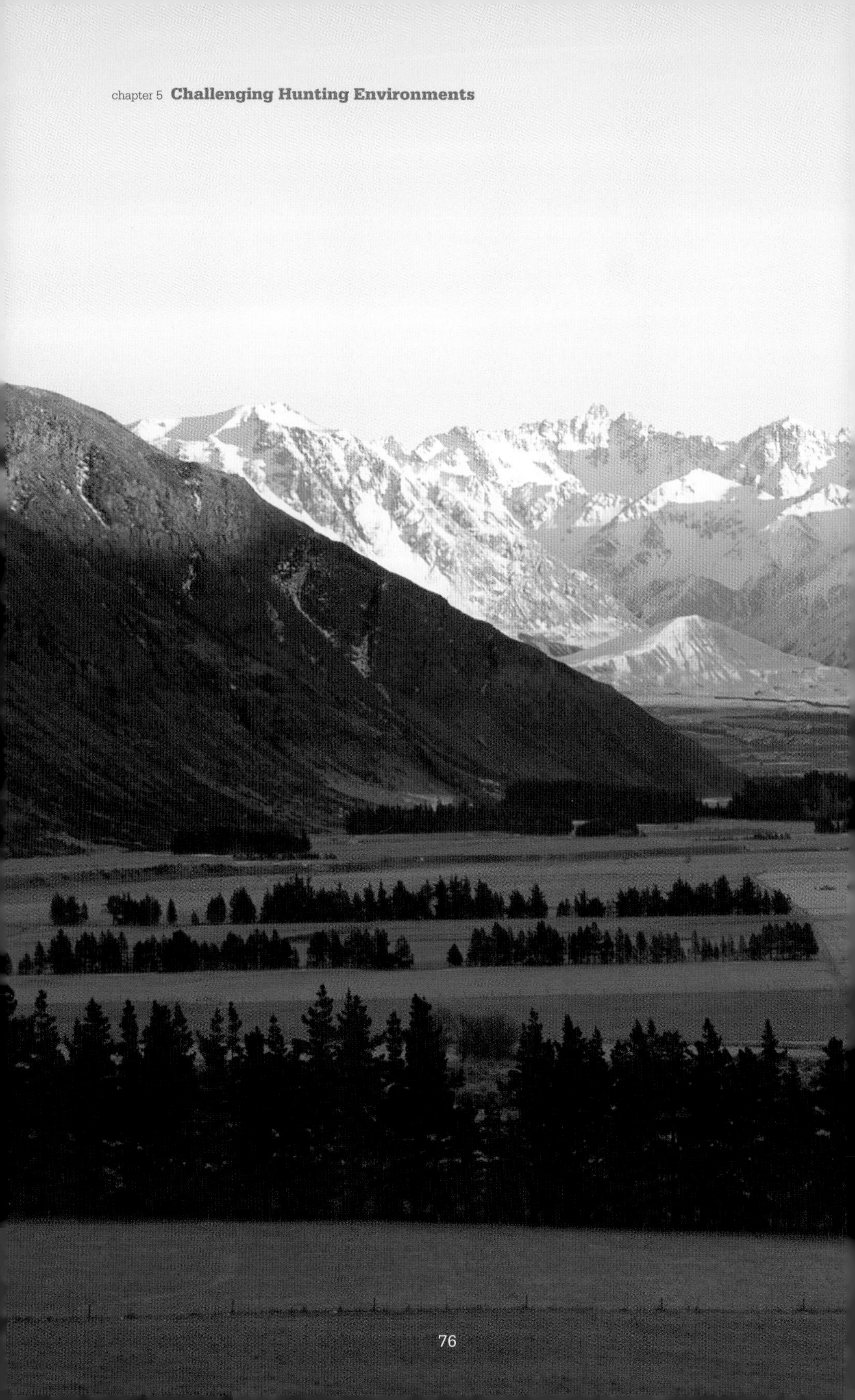

Calling the mountains *can be tough. Sight lines are limited, thermals can screw up a set and often the wind is simply swirling around the land masses. While there are lots of predators living in the mountains, it can be challenging to rustle them up.*

The bulk of material written about predator hunting is geared to the Great Plains hunter – and those that think calling in the mountains is the same have another thing coming.

mountain states. Even so, the bulk of material written about predator hunting is geared to the Great Plains hunter – and those that think calling in the mountains is the same have another thing coming.

While it is true the two types of hunting have similarities, mountain calling has its own unique set of calling techniques and styles not employed elsewhere.

Another notable difference is the variety of available species. Depending on which mountains you are in, it may be possible to call in fox (both grey and red), coyotes, bears, cougars and bobcats, all from one location. No other topography provides so much diversity for the opportunistic predator hunter.

Take Washington State for example. During the peak of the winter calling season, hunters have a good possibility of calling coyotes, bobcats, fox and the occasional cougar. Head to the same spot before winter sets in and you can throw bear into this mix as well. Where else can a predator hunter find such diversity? Washington is not the exception – most mountain states can boast this quality of hunting.

Techniques for Mountain Calling

Since the majority of mountains are covered by trees, underbrush sight lines and overall visibility are diminished when compared to hunting in open country. This lack of visibility makes mountain hunting more difficult. When predators have hidden approach routes and can circle downwind with impunity, not to mention enough cover to sit 50 yards away and watch the setup before committing to a final approach, a hunter's success is bound to decline.

To offset these challenges, mountain predator hunters must pick their stands very carefully and use every natural funneling obstacle to their advantage. For example, when I look for a spot to call in the mountains I focus on several key characteristics: the best possible sight lines, usually provided by a slight rise overlooking a valley or flat; a natural barrier that prevents predators from circling

Try to gain *as much elevation as possible when looking for a set in mountainous country. It will help with visibility as well as scent management.*

downwind, such as a cliff face, creek or river; or an open glade or clear-cut patch of timber. Once you establish the sight line, predict an approach pattern and limit the predator's options, you have done as much as you can to stack the odds in your favor.

Wind Direction

In addition to the curtailed view, wind direction can present a challenge. With swirling currents, updrafts and downdrafts, playing the wind can be a full time job. One trick is to use visible floating fibers to check wind direction. While commercially sold "wind indicating" powder gives hunters a good idea what the wind is do-

ing right around them (which in flat open places generally remains pretty constant) it disperses quickly and does not provide any indication what the wind is doing 50 or 100 yards away. Highly visible white or orange fibers, however, can give hunters a great idea where the wind swirls, dips or passes over a small depression, and provide a much more accurate picture of where a predator may catch an alarming smell.

In the mountains *you can often make several sets from one general area. Ridges and valleys block sound so it doesn't carry as far as it would on the open plains.*

Duration of Stay

When calling in the mountains I tend to stay in one position longer than I do in open country. To begin with, prime mountain calling stands are harder to find than good stands in open country, so when I do find one I like to milk it for all its worth. Also, in mountainous country it has been my experience that predators come to the call slower than they do in open country. This may be due to difficulty navigating thick terrain, hills and blow downs.

Finally, the biggest reason I stay in one place longer in the mountains is the increased presence of bobcats. While I have had bobcats come to call as quickly as a coyote, the vast majority of them come in really slow. Forty-five minutes to an hour is much more typical than the under-ten-minute appearances associated with coyotes. Since the mountains have bobcats and cougars and (depending on the state you are in) you can hunt them, it's often worth the wait. Giving predators more time will up your success rate more than anything else.

Choosing a Firearm

The diversity of predators in mountainous areas makes choosing a rifle extremely difficult. The size of the predators ranges from 15 pounds or so for a small bobcat to several hundred pounds for a large bear. While you can try to target various species with different calls, you can never be sure of what may come to the call. When you have a .17 Remington that is ideal for bobcats, you can bet your last dollar that a bear or cougar will come ambling down the ridge. When you go loaded for bear, rest assured a coyote will come trotting by. Trying to select the one perfect caliber rifle for hunting in the mountains is nearly impossible. For this reason I choose an all around rifle that I jokingly say is ill suited for any and all species that may come in. Most of the time this is a .243 Winchester. Loaded with quality expanding bullets it will work (although shot placement is critical) for bears. It is not too poorly suited for cougars, and kills coyotes and bobcats with ease – although with significant pelt damage. It truly is a jack of all trades and a master of none.

Another great option is to carry both a small caliber predator rifle and a large caliber handgun. This allows you to use a perfectly proportioned predator rifle (such as a .17 Remington, .17 Fireball,

.204 Ruger or one of the various .22 caliber centerfires on coyote, fox and bobcat), and also carry a firearm powerful enough to tackle a large, tough animal like a bear or cougar. I prefer anything in .44 mag on up to the .500 Smith and Wesson for revolvers and anything from .270 Winchester on up in T-C Encores.

Some hunters choose to scope their handgun. I prefer open sighted handguns and, since most shots on large game in the mountains is going to be less than 50 yards, feel more capable of making the shot with iron sights.

Picking a Call

I have used many hand calls for predator hunting in the mountains, but more and more I prefer electronic calls. To begin with, the sound quality on the new digital units is very good. Most electronic calls have a wide range of available sounds, including some large prey animals that are hard to duplicate with a mouth call.

> I have used many hand calls for predator hunting in the mountains, but more and more I prefer electronic calls.

Another reason I like electronic calls is that they can be remotely placed. When calling in mountain country, your overall visibility is restricted and there are many blind spots for a predator to sneak in. When you are calling by hand, a predator will often see your movement long before you see them.

Finally, I like remote calls for the safety factor. I realize the odds of a large predator (bear or cougar) attacking a caller may be slimmer than being struck by lighting, but I still feel better having the sound emanate from a brush pile other than the one I'm in.

Next to quantity and diversity, one of the biggest bonuses to mountain calling is the lack of pressure. There are far fewer predator hunters than in the Great Plains states – it is just not in the culture. For this reason, don't be afraid to pull out the old calls that have worn out their welcome in recent years. Standard cottontail-in-distress calls often work well, and most of the time no fancy calling is required.

Choose your stands carefully, be ready to wait awhile and start calling. You too may find your own Rocky Mountain high.

Hunting Eastern Coyotes

I also consider predator hunting east of the Mississippi a challenging condition. In my experience it is tougher to kill predators, especially coyotes, in the Eastern United States than it is in the West. I have written before that the biggest challenge hunters face when hunting the East versus the West is diminished sight lines. After hunting the East now for several years, it is more than the thicker country. I still believe the lack of visibility plays a vital role in making Eastern predators tougher to kill, but there are other factors at work as well.

> In my experience it is tougher to kill predators, especially coyotes, in the Eastern United States than it is in the West.

To begin with, the number of coyotes is not remotely close to what it is in the West. Oh sure, there are coyotes and by Easterner's standards there seem to be many of them with the population constantly increasing. However, from what I have seen the population density of coyotes in the East is not even close to their density in the West. I have no scientific data to back that up, it's just my impression from living and hunting across the West and in parts of the East.

Consider, for example, my current home in Wisconsin. I spend about an hour driving to work each morning and home in the evening. Ninety percent of the drive is through rural country, much of which is open pasture land or crop fields. In three years of making this drive five days a week in prime hunting hours, I think I have seen three coyotes and a couple of foxes.

Compare this to when I lived in western Nebraska and drove a similar distance through similar country. I saw that many coyotes every week. Heck, once in awhile I saw that many in a day! Aside from actual sitings confirming their existence, you just don't see the sign like you do in the West. I have hunted prime whitetail country across the Midwest and it is pretty rare to see fresh coyote tracks or scat. At night you only occasionally hear coyotes howling. Compare this to the West, where every trail and old two-track has multiple piles of coyote scat and lots of tracks. After a fresh dusting of snow, there are so many tracks it seems there must be a coyote behind every sage bush.

Hunting coyotes in timber, *which is so common in the East, is a difficult proposition. While there may be coyotes in the area, the brush and heavy tree cover makes it next to impossible to see them before they circle downwind and disappear. This one didn't quite make it.*

Over the last several years, I've convinced myself that the East as a general rule (I am sure there are exceptions) doesn't hold as many coyotes as the West. Now throw in the inherent difference in country, as well as predator behavior, and it becomes easy to see why it is so much tougher to kill coyotes in the East than in the West.

In the East, open space is generally agricultural fields. Often these fields have thick fence rows of brush and trees or are surrounded by woods. When this is the case, I have found that coyotes will invariably go the long way around to the caller through the timber, staying in cover until well downwind. As any predator hunter knows, this never works out well and the vast majority of predators, especially coyotes, smell the hunter and get out of Dodge long before they are seen.

> It seems that the majority of predators in Eastern areas are called and killed either at first light or after dark.

The final difference I've noticed is the distinct lack of activity in the daytime. I don't know why this is, but guess it may have to do with increased human activity. It seems that the majority of predators in Eastern areas are called and killed either at first light or after dark. I have spent entire days, from sun up to sun down, with perfect winter weather (overcast and cold, after a fresh snow) making set after set, not seeing a single coyote. In the West, on these types of days I have called coyotes throughout the day many, many times.

So what's a hunter to do? So far I've only told you how much tougher it is killing coyotes in the East versus the West, which I am sure a lot of Eastern hunters have suspected for a long time. So how do you tip the odds in your favor? Over the last few years I've figured out a few techniques that seem to help.

Multiple Hunters

In the West, I hunt the majority of the time by myself or with a single partner, and rarely wish we had a third. With a third hunter, it is more difficult getting into and out of sets and for most sets it is unnecessary. Generally speaking, two can adequately cover almost all of the surrounding country. In the East, however, this is not the case. The land is so broken with rolling hills or covered in trees, or has multiple approach routes that can't be seen from a single vantage point, that multiple hunters will actually up your bag considerably. When hunting the East, consider two hunters a minimum and three about ideal.

I have hunted many parts of heavily-timbered Wisconsin land where four hunters in a group wouldn't be too many. The key is to drop guys on likely approach points, especially on the downwind side. Have hunters carry a variety of rifles and shotguns, and place them where their tool fits the best. For this large party-type of hunting, it works best if one hunter is in charge, a kind of "hunt master" so to speak, and the others follow directions to avoid confusion.

Permanent Elevated Stands

This is a technique I started using in dense river bottoms along the North Platte River and found it works pretty well anywhere there is lots of cover. This is also a good technique if you want to hunt alone or don't have a large party of guys to hunt with.

I generally don't hang stands with predators in mind, but instead use my regularly deer stands. Since I hunt a considerable number of private farms I leave my stands up year around. In the winter when I am predator hunting I can choose between no less than 20 stands stretched over a 10-mile area. What I have found to work best is to use an electronic caller along with a decoy; this helps keep the predator's attention focused on the noise and not on movement in the treetops. Predators can pretty easily catch your movement in a stand, much more than I once thought possible. I don't know if it is the position of their eyes on their head or if they occasionally look for birds of prey or what, but I do know that it happens more frequently than with deer. For this reason, use stands that have good cover around them, such as pine trees that keep their cover year-round. I have also had good luck hunting out of elevated box blinds, which are common in the north woods. Since coyotes see them every day, they don't draw too much suspicion.

Remote Calling and Decoys

A remote electronic caller and a decoy help your odds, and this doesn't just apply to stand hunting. I use them in the East almost all of the time. Just getting the noise away from your position and adding some movement will help seal the deal on those predators that

The author *killed this coyote in Wisconsin in a relatively open pasture, even then the coyote nearly managed to sneak down wind using the available cover.*

manage to slip in undetected. In addition to drawing a predator's attention away from you, remote decoys and calling can help with downwind blind spots. By placing them in a certain way, even if the predator circles the calling you are in a position to intercept them on the downwind leg before they smell you.

Little Vocalization

In the West in the winter I use coyote vocalization a lot both for locating coyotes before I set up and for calling during breeding season. In the East I have observed a distinct lack of coyote response both in howling naturally as well as in response to a call. Once again, like so many of the mysteries of the East, I really don't have a solid answer for why this is, it's just been my observation. They will howl, and I have had decent luck locating packs at night, but it is rare to get them to sound off during the day. Unlike the West where you can pretty regularly get coyotes to howl back to a siren, this is not been my experience in the East. For this reason, as well as the much higher density of fox in the East, I don't howl very much. In the West I honestly don't think you hurt much by howling, whether you get a response or not. But in the East, where you are just as likely (if not more likely) to call in a red fox as you are a coyote, I think you hamstring yourself by sounding like a pack of coyotes in the area.

Different Types of Decoys and Calls

While there is no doubt that cottontails are a main source of food for predators in the East, I believe that Eastern predators have become more varied in their diets than their Western counterparts. Unlike much of the West, where mice and Jackrabbits probably comprise 90 percent of a predator's diet, in the East there is a whole smorgasbord of food to dine on. Rabbits, mice, game birds and road killed deer (much higher percentage than in the West) all contribute to a coyote's diet.

It seems that the massive explosion in turkeys and geese in the Midwest may be playing a significant part in a coyote's diet as well. It is common in the winter to see geese sitting by the thousands in corn fields, and there are enough wounded ones that make easy prey for fox, bobcats and coyotes. A hunting partner of mine, after seeing coyotes stalk his spread on more than more occasion while

Don't overlook *exploding populations of prey species as potential food sources. As goose populations have expanded, the likelihood of small predators taking them for food has also increased.*

goose hunting, decided to try a single sitting goose decoy with a combination of prey-in-distress calls and mournful honks from a call. He shot more coyotes that season than he ever had by any other method.

Stay Positive

One of the biggest tools an Eastern hunter can employ is to stay positive. It is easy to get frustrated in the East as you do not get rewarded as frequently as you do in the West. Pretty soon, especially if you are just getting started predator hunting, you begin to question your technique. Don't. Stay focused, know you are doing it right and keep making stands. Sooner or later you will kill a predator. Don't compare your success to folks in the West and don't benchmark your success on predator hunting videos, which are often filmed in serious coyote hotspots and have hours upon hours of non-producing stands edited out. Be patient, make as many stands as you can and hunt hard. That will eventually pay off whether you are east or west of the Mississippi.

CHAPTER 6

PREDATOR
HUNTING
IN SUBURBIA

I spent my early years predator hunting around my parent's rural western Washington home. At the time the area was comprised of old farms, timber company land and some National Forest. After returning from college, I noticed right away how drastically the country had changed in the four (or five'ish) years I was away. It seemed the Pacific Northwest experienced the dotcom boom like no other locale and my hunting ground was at the epicenter. In a few short years the old farms were gone, replaced by skateboard parks. The wooded areas had been turned into posh, multi-million dollar estates.

During that first fall of my return I was sitting around lamenting about the good old days with an old hunting buddy when I caught brown movement across the street in the underbrush. Previously a forest, the spot was now called an "environmentally friendly green space." The brown movement turned out to be a coyote.

The saying goes that cockroaches would be the only survivors after a nuclear holocaust. I think coyotes would be right there with the roaches. While blacktail deer and elk had moved into the mountains to escape suburban sprawl, the coyotes adapted. They were still there, living under a suburban skyline, hunting at night, choosing their prey like they always did. Despite the disruption of the wild places they seemed to be thriving.

This brief encounter sparked an idea; while the place had changed, the predator hunting probably had not. We made some phone calls and discovered we still knew some folks with property or access to property. We were out hunting old haunts the following morning.

After a short time at our first spot of the morning we quickly learned that things had changed. To our surprise, they had changed for the better.

Coyotes Thrive in Backyards

After checking local ordinances, my hunting partner and I accessed a patch of woods that was legal to hunt just outside the city limits. The property abutted a subdivision of homes that each sat on a few acres of semi-rural property – perfect coyote edge habitat. It was our theory that the coyotes were living in the one tract of woods and venturing into the subdivision at night looking for an easy meal.

Walking into our first stand our theory gained some strength. We had gone about 50 yards when my partner stopped and pointed to something with toe of his boot. At first I didn't recognize the twisted strip of plastic for what it was. Then I realized it was a cat's flea collar, gnawed in half at the back. Slyly smiling my partner said "Ol' Fluffy likely didn't chew that off himself."

Two steps further we found a pile of cat fur, two steps after that a pile of fresh coyote scat. Walking into that stand we counted no less than 10 piles of scat along the trail leading to the housing development. Obviously a nightly sojourn to town was a habit for these city dogs.

This is generally the case in suburbia where food is abundant. Outdoor house cats and small dogs get eaten regularly. Species like mice and rats thrive with an abundance of dog food in outdoor dog dishes and are protected by the convenient shelter in the crawlspace of houses. Rabbits also multiply uncontrollably in suburbia, as there is plenty of feed in small gardens and ornamental shrubbery,

> All in all suburbia creates a feast for predators, with little to no hunting pressure to make them wary.

With suburban sprawl, *predator hunters face new challenges. However, if done correctly there may be a pot of gold at the end of the cul-de-sac.*

and they breed like…well, you know. All in all suburbia creates a feast for predators, with little to no hunting pressure to make them wary.

> No coyotes are stupid, but city 'yotes are by far the least educated of the lot.

In that one woodlot we killed two coyotes that morning and took many more out of there over the years. While we killed them with all types of calls, an old Johnny Stewart tape recording of kittens in distress was always the most successful…go figure!

The point of this story is not so much about the meat and potatoes of calling coyotes in suburbia, that part is relatively easy. No coyotes are stupid, but city 'yotes are by far the least educated of the lot. They are used to human smells in a non-threatening environment, they have generally never heard a prey-in-distress call and, if they did have a "bad" run-in with humans it is more likely an old shoe was thrown at them instead of a 52 grain hollow point.

In the 'burbs you can get away with a lot more odor around a set and don't have to pay attention to the wind nearly as much as in the country. No, the trick in killing these coyotes is not the actual hunting and calling, it is more about finding the spots, avoiding conflicts with anti-hunters to keep those spots open and using the right tools for the job at hand.

Finding Spots

This type of hunting is not about knocking on doors and asking permission. Unlike ranchers who have seen a lamb killed by coyotes and will beg you to come out hunting, suburbanites are not so open to the idea. I remember one of my first and last door knocking experiences. Upon knocking, a soccer mom in a robe opened the door.

"Excuse me ma'am, I noticed you have quite a large wooded area behind your house. Would you mind if my brother and I coyote hunted out there?"

"Hunt?" with a slightly detached, puzzled look on her face, "…as in like *kill*?"

"Well, yeah hopefully that may happen if it all works out right."

With a look of revulsion and distaste she stammered, "Absolutely not!" and slammed the door.

I can't say I've tried knocking since that incident, but gauging from the responses of people I know living in suburbia, especially on the West coast, hunting regardless of species is not looked upon too kindly.

So you can generally forget about private property unless you know the people personally and they invite you on. But there are other options. Some parks may allow hunting. Sometimes large timber companies that own title to suburban land allow hunting. In many parts of the country there are still old school lands that have not been developed and are often legal to hunt. You just have to get a plat map and do your homework.

Over the years I've had some interesting success with land developers. I talked to a couple of developers who owned a several hundred acres that was not going to be developed for a few years. I asked permission to hunt and, while they were worried about liability, the actual hunting didn't bother them. One said, "I can't give you permission as my lawyers would come unglued over the liability of letting anyone on the property for any reason, but I absolutely don't care and no one is ever out there during the weekend." Then he winked. I hunted that property nearly every weekend for years and never had a problem. Old landfills that have been turned into green spaces may also provide an opportunity, provided they are decommissioned and open for public recreational use.

> You'll discover that a five acre patch of good cover is a stand, and a 40-acre patch can be heaven.

Over time, as you hone your skills, you will develop a nose for suburban hunting opportunities. You'll no longer be looking for the wide open vistas or ranches with tens of thousands of acres. You'll discover that a five acre patch of good cover is a stand, and a 40-acre patch can be heaven.

Know Your Laws and Local Ordinances

Suburban hunting is a bit trickier than out in the country when it comes to legality. In the country you need to check game laws, have the proper license, know the seasons and shooting hours and that is pretty much it. In suburban settings you have to pay more attention to laws about shooting within a certain distance of buildings and around schools, noise ordinances at night and "no shooting" or "no hunting" zones.

> If you are willing to put in the leg work and understand local ordinances, spend some time talking to local police to clarify their interpretation of laws and generally do your research, some phenomenal hunting can be the result.

Because it can get complicated very few people do it, which is why it is good hunting. If you are willing to put in the leg work and understand local ordinances, spend some time talking to local police to clarify their interpretation of laws and generally do your research, some phenomenal hunting can be the result.

As a side note, it is not a bad idea to print all applicable laws and local ordinances and keep them folded in a waterproof bag on your person while hunting. It is not uncommon for local law enforcement officers to not know the laws regarding hunting and discharging firearms in specific municipalities. In fact, if you are hunting around a small town it is not a bad idea to contact the local officer on duty ahead of time so he knows who you are and what you are doing in case he receives a call. Unfortunately, I found this out the hard way.

One night we were calling coons in a sweetcorn patch right on the edge of a small town, technically inside the city limits. The corn was just getting ripe and the coons were coming in droves. Since there was no hunting in the city, there was a large population of coons and as many as 25 of them at one time could be seen in the field during the cover of darkness.

The landowner, knowing we shot all kinds of predators and varmints, begged us to come take care of them one night, so we met with the chief of police. The farmer explained the situation and we explained our hunting technique and experience. In the end he saw that we were legal and weren't going to be unsafe and gave us an exception to hunt for that night.

It is a good idea *to not only know local laws before hunting suburbia, but to also consult with local law enforcement officials. Let them know exactly where and when you are planning to hunt, in case they get a call from a concerned homeowner.*

We went out and started calling with an electronic recording of a coon fight. We were calling for only a couple of minutes when a big old boar coon waddled in to investigate. I shot him with a load of BB's from my Benelli 12 gauge (we were using shotguns for safety reasons). It wasn't five minutes after the report had died down that blue and red lights lit up the skyline. It was obviously a police car and from the look of the lights it appeared to be getting closer. About the time I realized this, a police car shot over the hill and whipped into the field, his spotlight pinning us against the old barn we were sitting against, shotguns cradled in our laps. The car slid to a stop and out came an officer, shielded by his door, handgun trained on us. It was a scene straight out of COPS.

"Put your guns down!" he yelled across the field.

We immediately complied, then stood up to walk over to the officer to explain the misunderstanding. In retrospect, standing up probably wasn't the best idea as it sent the nervous officer into over-drive.

"Stop where you are!!" he shouted. "Get on the ground!"

Since his gun was still drawn and his voice was tenser than ever, we complied just slightly faster than immediately.

He then asked "What in the hell are you two doing?"

"Shooting coons..." was my partner's timid response.

"What?!?" the office sounded confused and unsure at our answer.

"Shooting raccoons in the corn patch. See there is a dead one over there."

After looking closer at our hunting gear, our shotguns, the electronic caller and the dead coon, he decided we weren't a threat and let us stand up.

"Well you must not know this field is inside the city limits so I am going to have to cite you for unlawfully discharging a firearm," he continued, now figuring he was just dealing with a couple of plain run of the mill morons, not homicidal maniacs.

"Wait a minute, we got permission from the chief of police just today."

Looking even more unsure, the office radioed back to dispatch.

"uh huh, yup, uh huh, alright, yes...I wish he would have told me that before I went on duty." From the side of the conversation we heard, the message must have got relayed, albeit a little to late.

Turning back to us the office said, "Ok then, I guess you guys are fine, go back to hunting."

Well needless to say after discharging one shell, having a police car storm into our set and then engage in a loud yelling match there was no point in calling anymore. But, aside from the coon, I did leave with something else that night: a valuable appreciation for letting the officer in the field know beforehand where you intend to be and what you plan to do.

Maintaining a Low Profile

When hunting suburbia I am ultra sensitive about remaining under the radar. This is for two reasons.

The first is just to keep my spots mine. Even though suburban areas are comprised primarily of non-hunters, there are still some hunters living there. If you make your spots and activities known it won't be long until other hunters are hitting your spots, and suburban hunting is not like ranchland USA that can handle tons of pressure. It has been my experience that other hunters will spoil a spot by not remaining under the radar from anti-hunters or they will burn it out through too much pressure. Either way the outcome will be the same and you will need to find a new spot.

The second reason I keep a low profile is to avoid non-hunter or anti-hunter attention. It is important to note that the reason I put so much effort into avoiding detection is not because anything I am doing is illegal. In fact, I am meticulous about checking all state, as well as local, ordinances. It is just not worth the hassle of dealing with some anti-hunters who can be unreasonable. I have seen more than one legal hunting area shut down by anti-hunting pressure. I have seen counties which were open to hunting suddenly enact a no-shooting ban because a few homeowners got vocal at a county meeting. For suburban hunting, it is best to stay as hidden as a coyote if you want it to last very long.

> For suburban hunting, it is best to stay as hidden as a coyote if you want it to last very long.

Suburban Camouflage

To maintain this low profile, take a look at your attire and change up accordingly. When suburban hunting, I play down my hunting clothes to what I like to call "granola-munching, hiker casual." While most suburbanites abhor the fact their pretty Persian got plucked off their deck by a coyote, they hate the thought of hunters nearly as much. By camouflaging your camouflage you can avoid a lot of problems.

Suburban predator hunters *may need to use different firearms than traditional predator hunters. Shown here are the .50 Dragon Slayer air rifle, a T/C Encore carbine with a Choate folding stock and a Mossberg 500 Shotgun.*

THE STEALTHY PACK WITH A FUNNY NAME

If you prefer to use a full size rifle or shot-gun over a handgun or carbine, pick a pack that not only masks your hunting purpose but completely hides a rifle. For this I love the Eberlestock Gunslinger. While it's avail-able in several camo and colored configu-rations, the all brown or all green model works fine for any hunting application and does not arouse suspicion in the field. Like any good pack it has tons of room to store calls, decoys and other hunting accessories, but best of all, it has an integrated rifle scabbard sleeve built in to the pack. This scabbard keeps the rifle close to the center of your back and pretty much completely con-cealed to the untrained eye. Also, the pack is expandable enough to put a dead coyote in a double layer of plastic garbage bags (tied at the top of course) and carry it out inside the main compartment to avoid detection.

Close up *of the Eberlestock Gunslinger pack with the integral scabbard for transporting a rifle. In this photo, it is shown with an Encore with a Choate folding stock. A large handgun or folding-stock rifle will completely disappear inside of the scabbard. With a full-stock rifle, the snap-on butt cover must be used to complete hide it.*

This coyote *was killed by the Author on private land in a suburban area. He had permission from the owner to be there.*

As much as I love Realtree, when I am going into areas where I can be seen by passing cars, housing developments or nature lovers out for a hike, I generally wear a set of tan or green Carhartt-style work pants and a solid green, tan or brown fleece jacket. If it is raining, Gore-Tex hiking-style rainwear in neutral colors will work fine for keeping you dry and hidden. To passersby you look like another hiker.

Also, take a look at your vehicle. Avoid an obvious hunting rig such as a lifted truck with hunting stickers plastered on the bumper and a gun rack in the window. For suburban hunting you won't be traveling off road, so the wife's car or the family SUV will work fine. As long as you can get permission to put a dead coyote in it, any vehicle will work. The less conspicuous the better.

Using Alternative Weapons

Suburban hunting often requires some extra thought regarding your choice of weapon. If I am using a centerfire rifle I stick to smaller calibers (like .17 Remington, .17 Fireball or a .22 Hornet) due to their low ricochet potential and diminutive report. Shotguns also have their place, as often the shots are close and ricochets are a non-issue.

> If noise is more of a concern than seeing people, take a look at bows, crossbows and (if they are legal) airguns.

If I'm hunting an area where I may run into people I carry a hiking-style backpack with my gear inside. This often includes a T/C Encore handgun with a 15-inch barrel. No one knows you have it and it works well for coyotes. If you still prefer a rifle over a handgun, look for an easily-hidden carbine model. The handiest suburban coyote rifle I have ever built is a super short T/C Encore in .223. I replaced the factory stock with a folding model by Choate and installed a .223 carbine barrel and a light weight bipod. When the stock is folded it can be stowed unobserved in any space an Encore handgun can, but it is as easy to shoot and as accurate as any rifle.

Pyramid Air
.50 Dragon Slayer

If noise is more of a concern than seeing people, take a look at bows, crossbows and (if they are legal) airguns. There are some super powerful air rifles on the market today. In fact, some are capable of handling many types of North American big game if ranges are kept within moderation, which makes them more than adequate for predator hunting. Some of these rifles available in large calibers include .30, 9mm, .457 and .50.

I recently tested the .50 Dragon Slayer by Pyramid Air and was impressed. Out of the box this gun will shoot one-half to one-inch groups at 50 yards all day long and produces over 200 foot pounds of energy – over two times that of a .22 long rifle with over twice the diameter of entry wound. A little custom work can bump up the foot pounds considerably. Although the Dragon Slayer is large and hard to conceal, what it lacks in compactness it makes up for in quietness (it is not much louder than a .22 short). In addition to being quiet, in many areas where shooting firearms is prohibited discharging an air rifle may not be. This does depend upon local ordinances, so know before you go.

> Suburban hunting can be fun, extremely productive and a unique challenge. But it is not for everybody.

After the Kill

After a predator is down things can get a bit dicey. Dragging a dead coyote through suburbia is not a good idea, but leaving a skinned carcass in the woods can be worse. A few years ago a skinned carcass, originally thought to be a domestic dog, was spotted laying in the woods by a local hiker. The local media quickly latched onto the story, speculating it to be everything from a demented person torturing people's dogs to a serial killer in the formative years to a religious cult celebrating under the dark of the moon. It turned out they were all wrong, it was just a skinned coyote left by a local hunter that received local as well as national media attention.

To avoid this kind of attention and hassle, I prefer to get the coyote out of the woods as quickly as possible in a concealed manner. If you choose a large enough pack, double bag the predator in question, tie off the top and pack him out inside the pack. Once out of the woods, I store them in a plastic tote (with a snap lock style lid) lined with cat litter. When placed in the back of a truck or SUV the tote will keep the carcass out of sight and the cat litter keeps the blood from running all over the place or out the back of a pickup bed. I skin them when I get home and dump the carcass on my own property where it will not draw attention.

Suburban hunting can be fun, extremely productive and a unique challenge. But it is not for everybody. It is not about beautiful open western vistas and solitude. It is not often easy to get access, and you will generally run into other people, some who may not like you or your sport very much. But it can be rewarding and with today's growing population of suburbanites it may be the only choice many of us have to hunt without traveling too far.

CHAPTER

7

COYOTE VOCALIZATION AND HUNTING THE RUT

"**O**ur area gets hit too hard, all of our coyotes are call-shy. They run when they hear a rabbit call."

If I've heard it once, I've heard it a thousand times, and in many cases it's true: Coyotes do get call-shy. I have even witnessed it myself. There is no doubt coyotes are one of the smartest, quickest learning, most adaptable animals in North America. It doesn't take too many close calls for them to realize that not all prey-in-distress sounds add up to an easy lunch. And if bullets clip their hair more than a couple of times, fooling them again is a tough task. A tough task, that is, if hunters don't change their tactics.

Back in my old coyote stomping grounds in western Nebraska, coyote hunting is nearly a religion, like ice fishing in the North and turkey hunting in the South. There are probably more predator hunters than there are deer hunters. And I have seen the same scene play out again and again: Sneak into an open canyon in the early dawn light and let loose with a rabbit-in-distress call. More often than not, coyotes will come out – out the opposite side running at full tilt for new territory. The wind was right, the approach was right, so what happened?

Those coyotes had been educated.

In areas like this, you sometimes have to prey on emotions rather than hunger to be successful. Sometimes you have to play to the romantic in a coyote, or possibly just their ego.

If you know what to say and how to say it, the coyote rut can be one of the best times of the year to hunt.

When the rut kicks in, whether for deer, elk or turkeys, powerful chemical reactions happen in the brain. As hunters, not only do we know this, we can capitalize on it and use it to our advantage. Many a swollen-necked buck has fallen to a well placed arrow because a scent trail was just too alluring to resist. How many turkeys get a lead surprise each season because they just had to have one more hen in their harem, and when was the last time you saw a big bull elk come in to a spike bugle just to socialize about the weather? The point is that the drive to reproduce can be a hunter's biggest ace in the hole - if he knows how to play his cards.

We all know mating season provides prime hunting opportunities for many prey species, but how does it work with coyotes? Luckily for predator hunters, all it takes is a little music and the right mood and you can be a predator hunting Don Juan.

Cash in on Pack Mentality

"Coyotes can and do vocalize all year, but the frequency and the response to vocalization increases slightly before, during and shortly after their prime mating months," says Eric Gese, Ph.D., Predator Researcher for Utah State University, USDA Predator Research Center.

Prime mating months run from early January until late February and are characterized not only by increased vocalization but also by pack behavior.

According to Gese, 90 percent of the time all of the breeding within in a pack is done by the alpha male and alpha female. Other subordinate coyotes in the pack, known as beta males and females, not only do not breed with each other, but are prevented from breeding at all and are kept in line by the alpha pair. Gese continues, "The vast majority of the time, coyotes are monogamous between the alpha male and female, but every once in a while one of the beta females will turn up with a liter of pups. In these cases, they usually are much smaller and less likely to survive than the alpha female's pups." Also according to Gese, "Packs vary in size from the breeding pair to up to ten or more depending upon region, but most typically hover around three or four, which are generally comprised of the alpha male and female pair along with a couple of yearling offspring of either sex."

> According to Gese, 90 percent of the time all of the breeding within in a pack is done by the alpha male and alpha female.

Once a pack establishes a territory they will defend it vigorously against all intruders, especially the nomadic males and females which have been pushed out of other packs. These lone coyotes will roam the country looking for unclaimed territory to take up residence. If they hit on an area that has little scent, no visible scratch marks and no response to howling, it quickly becomes home sweet home.

This behavior can be used to your advantage when setting up a stand. If a pack is already in residence they won't hesitate to defend their territory from a nomadic coyote.

Mating pairs and small packs will defend their territory vigorously when mating season arrives. But territories are large and determining if a pack of coyotes is in the vicinity of your calling station can be difficult. Use a whistle or siren to locate the pack before calling. If you just sit down and start howling, one of two things generally happens. Either coyotes respond immediately and you are not ready for their approach, or they show themselves at several hundred yards, sit down and wait to see who the interloper is. If you use a loud electronic siren instead of a howl, coyotes will generally sound off but not come running – much like the difference between get-

> Mating pairs and small packs will defend their territory vigorously when mating season arrives.

ting a turkey to shock gobble in the spring versus getting a response from a hen yelp. In the first situation the gobbler is just sounding off, in the second, he is often on his way towards your position.

By knowing where they are, about how many are in the pack and how far away they are, you leave yourself the option to either set up and call them in or relocate to a better spot before calling.

Different Season, Different Diet

During the breeding season, food sources may change depending on the region. Since breeding season occurs in the middle of winter in many parts of a coyote's range, there may be deep snow. Larger animals (including livestock) may become prey when the packs increase in size and mobility for large mammals gets more difficult. There is nothing wrong with using deer and elk-in-distress calls during this time of the year, as well as electronic recordings of livestock (especially sheep, goats and pigs) in distress.

In addition to changing your calling strategy, now is a great time to hunt around natural food sources. Many times in the middle of winter I have set up near dead livestock and road-killed deer (that had been moved and subsequently worked over by coyotes) and started howling. When there is a large food source available, coyotes will often eat their fill and drift off a short distance away to rest. Forget about enticing them in to a rabbit-in-distress call, another coyote invading their territory and food larder is sure to bring them running.

When the rut *kicks in, don't feel like you have to call constantly. Many hunters do well by calling infrequently and waiting. Find a comfortable place to sit that blocks your profile and wait them out. The results may surprise you.*

Decoys Get Their Bristles Up

One of the surest ways to get an alpha male's bristles up is to use a coyote decoy to visually confirm what his ears are telling him.

The times I've howled coyotes in during mating season, they responded to calls with like calls, then ascended to a high vantage point to survey their territory. From there, they sat and stared over the countryside for up to 30 minutes scanning every bush for a sign of the invading coyote. Often they will come to investigate even without a visual confirmation. However, there are always a few who hang up until they see something worth investigating. Then there are those who scan and scan until they see a glint of a barrel, a shine of scope or an uncomfortable hunter reposition himself to relieve a sleeping leg – and the game is up. With a coyote decoy skylighted off to one side of the caller, you can tip the odds in your favor and lure more of those suspicious coyotes into range.

> One of the surest ways to get an alpha male's bristles up is to use a coyote decoy to visually confirm what his ears are telling him.

BREEDING SEASON VARIANCE

The peak of the breeding season is difficult to pin down. According to Eric Gese, Ph.D., Predator Researcher for Utah State University, USDA Predator Research Center, "Much of it depends on region. Like whitetail, coyotes in northern environments seem to come into their peak breeding cycle earlier than those in southern regions." That being said, regardless of where you find them, coyotes start breeding in December and generally finish up by the end of February. While the actual breeding may not be going on, from a caller's standpoint the pre- and post-rut time periods of November and March can also be good times to call, with increased natural vocalization and territorial tendencies.

If using electronic calls, *use them remotely. Coyotes sneak in to survey a situation. By not having the call emanate from your location, you stand a better chance of not being seen.*

Conversing with Coyotes

The biology and theory behind coyote vocalization is well documented and understood, but putting it into effect when hunting is often a different story. When I first started using vocalization, it was hard to resist switching back to more traditional prey sounds. It was a hunt with Mark Zepp that completely sold me on the effectiveness of vocalization.

Zepp and I were hunting one perfect January day when we set up on a ridge overlooking an expansive desert valley. We had no luck all morning and Zepp suggested I try howling. "Why not?" I thought, nothing else was working. I howled once, then followed it up with a short bark. When I went to howl again, Zepp whispered, "Just sit tight and see what happens." I did as instructed. We waited for several minutes and nothing happened. Just when I was going to try it again, a howl resounded from small crease in the valley floor several hundred yards away. This howl set off multiple other howls from all directions. Zepp just smiled.

119

"Don't do a thing," he hissed. The howls drifted off in the morning stillness and again all was quiet – I was about jumping out of my skin I wanted to howl again so badly. After several more minutes of silence, a set of ears poked over the far ridge, moving in our direction. Right behind them another set followed. A pair of coyotes became visible as they slunk through the grass and sage looking for who was howling in their territory. I never made another peep, but the coyotes slowly worked their way to less than 100 yards of our position, scanning for invaders the entire time. When the shooting was over, both lay dead before us.

What to Say

Later that night at dinner we discussed the day's events. We had killed several coyotes and never blew a rabbit call. Vocalizing was extremely effective if one just knew what to say. "Vocalization actually comes in several forms," Zepp elaborated. "It is not as simple as just howling. It includes male challenge barks, female invitational barks, lonesome howls, pack howls and pup-in-distress calls." These are just the basics and the ones most hunters use – undoubtedly there are many other sounds coyotes use to communicate with each other. All of these noises can be made with mouth calls but, unlike rabbit calling, it does take practice to get it right and sound realistic. One false call and you may turn them running in the opposite direction.

Good methods for learning to vocalize with coyotes include listening to professional recordings on tapes or electronic callers and paying attention in the wild. Next time you are out hunting and coyotes start howling, just sit back and really listen. You will hear not only the standard howl, but all manners of yips, barks and short howls.

If you can't master the mouth call, rest assured that many of today's electronic calls have extremely good recordings of coyote vocalization. In the case of digital callers, realistic custom sounds can often be downloaded from the internet.

When to Talk

When to use vocalization is a big part of the equation. Luckily, vocalization will work in one form or another throughout much of the year.

Early in the season, pup-in-distress calls work nicely. The family packs are still together and a female will respond quickly to what she perceives to be a wounded or threatened pup. I have had pup-in-distress calls work year around, and especially when coyotes are still in small to medium sized groups.

As winter progresses, lonesome and pack howls help to locate coyotes and bring them in when territory lines are crossed.

As winter turns to early spring and breeding season begins, male challenge and female invitational calls bring coyotes of both sexes running to either start pairing up or defend their territory.

Dan Thompson, noted coyote caller, ADC hunter and call manufacturer, elaborates on the subject. "The most productive time I have found over the years is in the early fall before the deer hunting season starts. By this time, the pups are out hunting on their own, but the family unit is often still together. The mothers are very protective and will respond to a pup-in-distress call extremely well. Often during this time of the year you will call several coyotes in at the same time. Even after you shoot, if you hit a pup-in-distress call, you can get an opportunity at killing multiple dogs."

> Early in the season, pup-in-distress calls work nicely. The family packs are still together and a female will respond quickly to what she perceives to be a wounded or threatened pup.

How Much to Say

This is probably the biggest failing of most predator hunters (myself included) – not knowing when to shut up. Coyotes don't take much vocalization. Thompson agrees, "The biggest key to calling coyotes is picking your time and knowing what to say. To begin with, most guys over-use vocalization – a little goes a long way and a lot often messes up the whole deal."

Unlike using a prey-in-distress call, where most callers call at regular intervals with relatively set breaks, when using coyote vocalization, respond to what the coyotes are doing and how they are acting. When you get a response with a howl, bark or pup-in-distress call, don't do any thing else. The odds are that the coyote is going to come find you. If you have a visual on the coyote, do nothing more unless the coyote decides to leave. As long as he is sitting in one spot or coming closer the best plan is to stay silent.

Coming in to Watch the Fight
One thing that's true about a fight is that people will stop and watch. The same is true for coyotes. I have had tremendous success over the years using a whipped coyote call or simply making distressed coyote sounds on an open reed howler. I've seen this call work wonders, from convincing wary coyotes to come running, to keeping a pack together and on site even after the shooting began, allowing the hunters to kill multiples out of the pack. The point is, a whipped coyote sound is a valuable call during this time of year and it should never be far from reach. While I don't recommend opening sets with it, if coyotes hang up go to it immediately. Once the shooting starts and there is more than one coyote in the area, have it cued up on the electric call and hit it immediately at full blast.

> One thing that's true about a fight is that people will stop and watch. The same is true for coyotes.

Throw Away the Rabbit Call?
After reading this some hunters may wonder why more callers don't utilize vocalization. There are a couple of answers.

To begin with, vocalization is a bit tougher to learn than standard predator calling, and the learning process can be a bit slow. Until electronic calls hit the market in easy-to-use, lightweight packages, the only good option was to use a mouth call, which took significant practice and a certain amount of skill.

The second reason is just plain stubbornness. Many a coyote has been killed using rabbit-in-distress sounds. When it doesn't work,

Taro Sakita, *Washington State predator hunter, uses mouth calls and electronic calls interchangeably to vocalize with coyotes.*

hunters just figure there were no hungry coyotes in the area. Few stop to consider that there may be plenty of coyotes in the area, but they're just too smart to be fooled.

The final reason more hunters don't use vocalization is because they have tried without success. This lack of success may be due to improper calling, the wrong sound or using it at the wrong time of year. Or maybe everything was right, and there were just no coyotes

Electronic calls and traditional *howlers are available to communicate with coyotes. Both work well, but electronics offer the novice caller a significant advantage.*

in the area. For whatever the reason, most hunters are not willing to experiment and will stick with "proven" methods regardless of the results.

Should hunters throw away rabbit calls entirely? Not hardly. They always have and probably always will be the mainstay of the predator hunter's arsenal. That doesn't mean when the time is right, one shouldn't howl now and again just to see what might happen.

Coyote Howlers

The biggest mistake novice predator callers run into when learning vocalization is not having the right tools for the job. I have said many times that there is not really a right or wrong way to call coyotes using a standard prey-in-distress call, as an animal in distress is not trying to communicate. When vocalizing with coyotes, quite the opposite is true. Coyote vocalization is complex, and realistic sound is the key to success. The calls I have used and recommend are as follows:

Thompson

Dan Thompson's Red Desert Howler has become one of the most widely used howlers in the industry simply because it works. Loud, realistic sound combined with versatility make this a must-own call. I also like his brass cartridge, pup-in-distress call. While not as loud or versatile as the Red Desert Howler, it makes one of the most realistic pup-in-distress calls I have ever heard.

Zepp

While Thompson may be the master, Zepp isn't far behind and his calls are also first-class. I use his 1080 and it is extremely effective. While it is not technically classified as a howler, the 1080 has interchangeable reeds and sounds very realistic when used as either a prey-in-distress call or howler. If a hunter is looking for one call to do a variety of jobs really well, the 1080 is hard to beat.

Sniper Styx Howler

I really like the easy-to-blow, natural sounding characteristics of the Sniper Styx Classic Buffalo Horn Howler. This call is made from injection molded polymer, which is easier to make consistent than natural material, and it sounds just as good. This is an excellent long range howler to keep in your pack.

FOXPRO

I use the FOXPRO FX 5 regularly for several simple reasons: it sounds great, it is extremely loud, it is capable of making a wide-range of different coyote vocalizations (many of which are hard to do with a mouth call) and it is easy to use. However, the most practical reason I use an electronic call is because it performs regardless of conditions. Winters in the West can be frigid cold and when it is below zero for most of the day mouth calls can freeze up if they are not kept inside your jacket. Electronics (while they may have a shorter battery life in the cold) will almost always work with no parts to freeze up.

8

PREDATOR RIFLES

P redator rifles come in all shapes and sizes. Some hunters prefer bolt actions, others like semi-autos, still others prefer the simplicity and reliability of a single shot. When it comes to predators, there really are no right or wrong answers. It is all about what you like, what works best for your shooting style and what you are comfortable with. While the following discussion is by no means a complete list, it covers rifles in the categories most often associated with predator hunting and outlines specific models and features I find useful in the field. Again, there is no right or wrong answer here. A predator rifle is what you have in your hands when a predator comes a-callin'. In some cases a precision bolt rifle may be ideal, other times the quick follow up potential of a semi-auto may be just what the doctor ordered. In the end the choice is yours and only you can decide what is right for your hunting situation.

Semi-Auto Predator Rifles

I am not a "techy" guy, but a traditionalist. I believe the fragrance of Hoppe's should be bottled for aftershave. I like the looks of a deeply finished walnut stock with a figure so complex you go cross-eyed staring at it. And I am nuts about a rich blue job, you know the kind where it is so blue it looks purple and still wet? In short, I like guns to look like guns. But I am also smart enough to know when one tool accomplishes a task better than another for the job at hand. It was this realization that made me swallow my pride

Coyote rifles
come in many action types, but most traditionalists still use bolt actions.

and accepting an AR as a viable hunting tool.

It was close to 15 years ago when I first carried an AR-15 afield for coyotes. I hated the looks of them, but I started using this rifle for the simple fact that it worked and worked well. It was chambered in what I still believe to be one of the best coyote calibers around, the .223 Remington. The rifle itself was extremely accurate and worked under all sorts of conditions. Best of all, I really didn't care if it got scratched, dented, dinged or rusted. To me it held about as much sentimental value as the shovel and tire chains behind the seat of my pickup.

Back then, few carried black guns for predators. I got my fair share of strange looks from local ranchers and even stranger questions from my hunting partners. In addition to the obvious flags it raised in the looks department, many folks doubted the accuracy, reliability, and overall function of a semi-auto rifle as a hunting tool, especially one to be used in dirty, dusty and cold conditions so often encountered predator hunting. Today, as anyone who keeps up with ARs can tell you, those questions have pretty much been put to rest. Those who have used AR-style rifles realize that they are very accurate, on par with most bolt actions, reliable and unsurpassed in terms of ruggedness.

AR-15s and their numerous variants can make excellent, albeit non-traditional, predator rifles. Most are accurate, reliable and durable. This Armalite is equipped with a night scope to call predators around the clock.

Since my first experience with these guns, AR customizers have captured even more of the hunting market with camo dipped accessories, easy scope mounting options, stocks that remain warm to the touch for cold weather hunting, extra large trigger guards and drop-in target-style triggers.

It's no secret to most predator hunters that the AR-15 style of rifle can be customized into a near ideal predator rifle. Now it seems that everyone is realizing, simultaneously, that there is a market for a factory produced version. Possibly the biggest "legitimizer" of the AR as a hunting rifle came about from an unlikely source: Big Green. When Remington unveiled its newest centerfire offering, the R-15 VTR, it was a shock for many to learn that it was a hunting colored AR variant.

But Remington is not alone in its quest to modify the trusted military arm into a hunting platform. Several companies are now offering ARs with custom features as well as field-tested refinements that all benefit the hunter. To see what has changed from yesteryear, I took several of these factory hunt-ready ARs into the field and put them through their paces.

Remington R-15 VTR

It is apparent at first glance that this rifle is built for the field. The biggest difference hunters see right off the bat with Remington's intro into the "black gun" market is that is no longer black. To make it more effective in the field, as well as reduce some of the downcast stares from non-AR shooters, they softened the look with a full Realtree Max 1 camo dip. Not only are the results effective for predators, but the overall look is fantastic.

Underneath the dip, the R-15 VTR is a pretty standard, target-grade AR. The barrel is 20 inches of matte blued fluted carbon steel with a slight target recessed crown. The full-sized A4 stock is comfortable and provides a place for extra gear such as a small cleaning kit or, for serious predator hunters, extra batteries for flashlights or even a small game call. Out of the box my R-15 had a reasonably crisp trigger that broke around 4.5 pounds. There was a little overtravel, and some pre-break creep, but nothing that couldn't be cleaned up by a competent gunsmith or a drop in replacement trigger such as by JP.

The flat top design is essential on any AR designed to handle a full sized rifle scope with a medium to large objective lens. You don't need iron sights on a predator rifle so why fuss around with them – the Remington comes sans

The Remington R-15 *is an excellent hunt-ready AR-style rifle. Fluted barrel, good quality trigger and Realtree camo dip make this rifle stand apart from the AR crowd.*

sights and no front mounting block. In fact, should users ever wish to easily install iron sights they are out of luck. But since this gun is designed for predator hunting, the need for iron sights is pretty miniscule.

Smith and Wesson M&P

The Smith and Wesson M&P obviously traces its linage back to a law enforcement and military background. Many of the features required for those uses also serve extremely well for hunters. A soft, finger-grooved rubber rear grip partnered with a skeleton stock covered in foam helps keep weight down while maximizing comfort. The free-floating aluminum hand guard is extended in length, offering more room for the non-shooting hand even when a bipod is installed. These little features, while only a small part of the overall package, really do count in the field, making the M&P an effective hunting rifle.

The M&P sports a target-crowned, stainless steel bull 20-inch barrel with a bead-blasted matte finish to reduce glare. The model I tested, like the other two test models in the group, was set up for a scope with a flat top receiver sans front or rear sights. However, unlike the Remington, the M&P could be swapped over to iron sights by mounting them to the flat top rear base and front sight base.

The trigger is a two-stage, military-style trigger that was pretty clean while still being safe for use with gloves in cold weather. It broke right around the four pound mark, but was crisp with out excessive over travel. To those unaccustomed to two-stage triggers, there may seem to be excessive travel before the sear disengages, but once users are familiar with the takeup, it's apparent how well they can perform.

Rock River Arms Coyote Rifle

This is the only rifle of the group that readily acknowledges its intended purpose – predator hunting. And of the group it was my immediate favorite out of the box as it has some great features. Like the other two rifles, it had a flat top receiver with no sights. Like the M&P, it had a front mounting block so iron sights could be installed if desired. It had a grip structure similar to the Smith and Wesson M&P, which I prefer. The semi-custom pistol grip and skeleton stock made for a great combination, especially when combined with the rubber-coated Hogue free-floating hand guard, which is factory equipped on the Coyote Rifle. The barrel is a 20-inch matte blued model with a flash suppressor.

The biggest advantage of the Rock River over the other two models is the oversized trigger guard. ARs traditionally have a relatively small trigger guard opening and when combined with heavy winter gloves it can be tight at best. The Rock River Coyote Rifle utilizes a uniquely formed lower trigger guard plate that significantly opens up some extra room.

Out of the box, the trigger on this rifle was phenomenal. It is a traditional military style two-stage trigger with a very definite takeup and secondary stop. Once used to it, it is not

Another great hunting style AR *is the Rock River Arms Coyote. Note the extra large trigger guard, flat top receiver and Hogue grips and forend.*

only relatively safe, but easy to use. Once the takeup is removed, it broke clean at just over three pounds with very little perceptible creep and only minor over-travel – by far the best of all the triggers tested.

Thoughts on Barrel Twist

My first .223 years ago was a 1:14 twist that would barely stabilize stubby 40-grain bullets. Many rifles were twisted 1:12, which works well for a wide range of bullet styles in the 55-grain weight category. What designers have found is that a faster 1:9 or 1:8 twist will still shoot lightweight, lower BC (ballistic coefficient) predator bullets as well as a slower twist, but can handle the heavier (up to 80 grain), high BC, VLD bullets as well – something the slower twists cannot do. It is important to note that all of the rifles as tested came from the factory with fast twist barrels (either 1:8 or 1:9).

What does this mean for predator hunters? For most, unfortunately not much, as they are shooting factory fodder with light-weight frangible bullets with low BC, but it does make a difference for handloaders. For this group who know the downrange potential of heavier bullets with a high BC (especially at longer ranges) or for hunters wishing to tackle game larger than coyotes and want a heavier bullet for penetration, they can custom-tailor a load with a much wider spectrum of bullets than a hunter shooting a rifle with a slower rate of twist. Granted, the ultimate benefits are sometimes limited by the overall length of the cartridge that can be loaded in the magazine, but the faster rates of twist will still stabilize a wider range of usable bullet weights.

Testing

Since all ARs are similar in design I based my tests on several quantifiable results, such as out of the box accuracy, trigger pull and reliability with factory ammunition.

At the range, all rifles loaded and functioned the same, and I used one magazine to isolate or minimize any chance of feeding problems using different components.

All of the guns functioned flawlessly. Unlike AR-15s of a generation ago where GIs bitterly complained about their lack of reliabil-

	Remington R15 VTR	Rock River Arms Coyote	Smith & Wesson M & P
Barrel length	20″	20″	20″
Rate of twist	1 in 9″	1 in 9″	1 in 8″
Overall length	38.5″	38.5″	38.5″
Overall weight	7.8 lbs	8.4 lbs	7.8 lbs
Trigger	4.5 lbs	2-stage match	2-stage match
Best 3-shot group	.92″	.68″	.85″
Misfeeds/malfunctions	none	none	none

ity, modern ARs function just fine. I tested a variety of both factory new ammunition (both premium hunting loads and standard plinking fodder) as well as good quality remanufactured ammunition, and experienced not a single failure to feed or extraction or ejection problem. I am sure with some ammunition or hard field use and lack of proper cleaning some jams would crop up. But if kept clean and fed well, cycling problems seem to become a non-issue.

In the accuracy department, all of the guns shot extremely well. It used to be a heck of a bolt action rifle that would keep its bullets under an inch at a hundred yards, but all of the ARs tested did it just fine with at least one style of hunting ammunition.

Keep in mind all rifles were tested with factory ammunition and I am sure a little with a little tweaking with handloads the results could be further improved.

Semi-Autos: Conclusion

All of the rifles performed admirably, with a slight accuracy edge going to the Rock River Coyote rifle. In addition to being a good shooter, it also had other features I liked such as the skeleton stock, rubber covered hand guard, large trigger guard and soft pistol grip.

If I could make some changes I would lose the flash hider and dip the whole gun or at least key accent pieces in Realtree Max 1, much like the Remington. Not only do I like this look, I feel it gives a hunter an advantage at staying hidden and helps non-black gun folks truly see what these rifles can do without letting preconceptions get in the way.

Day in and day out
*bolt action rifles are
taking down predators,
and it's no surprise.
They are chambered in
a wide array of calibers,
are accurate and most
western big game
hunters are accustomed
to their use.*

Bolt Action Predator Rifles

While shotguns, handguns, semi-automatic rifles, muzzleloaders, and maybe even sling shots and spears, have at one time or another played a part in the predator hunter's arsenal, one thing remains a constant – a good ole bolt action rifle.

Shotguns are for when predators are up close and moving fast. Semi-auto rifles are perfect when a quick followup shot may be needed, and handguns are ideal when we are feeling a bit too over-confident and need to be brought down a notch. But while these types of firearms are filling niches, the traditional bolt action is piling up predators, day in and day out.

One of the biggest benefits *of a bolt action rifle is the range of calibers for which it is chambered straight from the factory. In the rare event you can't find your pet caliber available in a factory rifle, it is easy to get most bolt actions rebarreled to suit your needs.*

Bolt actions work and they work well. Most bolt action rifles are capable of accuracy that makes them desirable for hitting small targets such as predators. Aside from accurate, they are reliable. Come sand, snow or freezing rain, the odds are the bolt is going to work as good as anything and a far sight better than some things.

Also, they are chambered in a variety of calibers ideal for predator hunting. You can find a factory bolt action chambered in everything from a diminutive .17 Remington fireball to the .257 Weatherby Magnum and every commercial cartridge in between. Best of all, bolt actions are instinctive to most of us. The action of cycling a bolt, switching of a side mounted safety and dumping a floor plate is something most of us have done many, many times making it second nature. Of all the great bolt action rifles designed for predator hunting, here is what to look for when picking one.

Accuracy

A predator rifle has to be accurate first and foremost. I like to have confidence in my rifle and know it will do its part if I do my part. The good news is with bolt actions, 90 percent of them come from the factory in this state and those that don't can usually be turned around pretty quickly with a bedding job and some handloads. If they don't come around after that, I would suggest unloading it to someone who likes projects and start over. The basic law of bolt action averages suggests it is next to impossible to get two duds back to back.

Ease of Handling

I prefer a bolt rifle to be easy to handle, light weight and have good pointablity. This wasn't always the case and I've owned my fair share of bull barreled, benchrest-styled monstrosities. But I've walked a lot of miles since then and now prefer a lighter rifle. For predator hunting start with a short action, one designed for the caliber, choose a cartridge that does well with a barrel on the short side (something in the 22 inch range is ideal) with a medium taper and look for a stock that is rigid, but not overly built. You will find that, when calling, probably 80 percent of all predators are shot at around 100 yards. 10 percent are closer and 10 percent are further

> While shotguns, handguns, semi-automatic rifles, muzzleloaders, and maybe even sling shots and spears, have at one time or another played a part in the predator hunter's arsenal, one thing remains a constant – a good ole bolt action rifle.

Bolt action rifles *are ideal for taking long range, unhurried shots. When you are set up properly with a bolt action rifle, a second shot is seldom needed.*

away. While you may pick up a few more of those long range coyotes with a bull barreled target style rifle, you will probably miss just as many of the close running ones as well. In the end it will equal out. Since it does, I prefer to carry a lighter rifle.

Other Predator Touches

Another touch I like on a bolt action rifle is a detachable box style magazine, but to be honest most of my rifles don't have it. Most of mine have a traditional hinged floor plate. This obviously works fine for me as I tend to use it all the time, but a couple of my rifles have a drop magazine and every time I use one of them in the field I think, "gee, that's a good idea, why don't all rifles have that?" The simple fact is that predator hunting is not like big game hunting. When hunting big game, I leave the truck, load my rifle and walk all day before heading back to the truck at dark. The difference between a hinged floor plate and a drop magazine doesn't make one iota worth of difference to me in this situation. But when predator hunting, I get out of the truck and make a stand for maybe 30 minutes. Then I head back to the truck, unload the rifle, drive to a new spot (sometimes only a mile away over a dirt two track), get back out of the truck, load the rifle, etc. I may do this a dozen times in a day. Individually loading a drop floor plate rifle each time gets to be a pain, which is why I prefer a box style magazine in these situations.

I also prefer synthetic stocks on a predator rifle. They stand more abuse, don't scratch as easily and best of all are not affected by moisture like a wood stock can be. While I like the looks of wood, for a day in day out working rifle it is hard to beat synthetic. If you can't bring yourself to embrace plastic, try a laminate. They are nearly as durable as synthetic and look a whole lot better.

> While I like the looks of wood, for a day in day out working rifle it is hard to beat synthetic.

The final touch I like on a predator rifle is a non-rusting metal finish. This can be one of the several aftermarket finishes available which reduce corrosion or it can be a camo dip finish. For the same reason I like box magazines, I like protective finishes. Predator hunters often subject their rifles to hot and cold temperatures all day long by getting in and out of trucks. This shifting of temperature can easily lead to condensation, which quickly leads to rust. In my opinion the more protection the better when it comes to predator rifles, and having a matte black or camo finish doesn't hurt in keeping them hidden either.

If you have *the option, buy a predator rifle with a detachable magazine. It is money well spent and will make your life easier.*

It seems that everything in the sport of predator hunting has become refined, improved or specialized in the last decade and rifles are no exception. It wasn't that long ago that a predator rifle was any rifle chambered in a small, centerfire caliber. While most manufacturers still make a wide variety of rifles chambered for smaller cartridges on smaller actions, only a few are making a true predator rifle with features a predator caller will appreciate. Here is a quick rundown of some of the rifles worth considering for the predator hunter.

Remington Model 700 VTR Desert Recon

The Model 700 has a fine reputation among shooters worldwide. It is accurate, dependable, and available in a wide range of calibers and models to suit any need. Over the years several models have been employed by predator hunters with good results, and recently Remington introduced another fine offering that will make predator callers swoon. It is the VTR (Varmint Tactical Rifle) Desert Recon.

The Remington VTR *is an ideal rifle for the predator caller. The triangular-shaped barrel, synthetic stock, matte finish and high tech camo pattern make it as unique as it is functional.*

The first thing hunters will notice is the techy but functional tan digital camo stock. This stock with its soft overmold grip panels is not only functional for a predator rifle that will see hard use in the field, but blends in well with natural surroundings. Combine that with the matte black metal and this is one rifle that won't spook game.

The next major change for Remington is the innovative barrel design. The triangular contour combined with the integral muzzle brake has been extensively tested to increase accuracy as well as decrease cooling time. While the cooling time is not a major factor for low volume predator hunters, it is a nice feature if the rifle is going to pull double duty as a high volume prairie dog rig as well. This rifle is available in .204, .223 and .22-250.

Winchester Model 70 Coyote Light

The Winchester Model 70 Coyote Light reaches the upper range of weight I prefer to carry in the field. Based on their standard Coyote rifle released several years ago (which was too heavy for my liking), the Coyote Light is nearly the same rifle without the extra weight. The barrel, while medium-heavy, is fluted to reduce weight and the Bell & Carlson carbon fiber stock has been ported to do the same. Inside the stock resides a CNC machined aluminum bedding block to provide a solid bedding platform for increased accuracy. My own Coyote Light is an amazingly accurate gun, although seems finicky about bullets. With most offerings it will stay under an inch at 100 yards. Depending upon caliber, this is one rifle that can pull double duty as a predator rifle and a long range varmint gun. The Coyote Light has been offered in several caliber configurations over the years, but is now being offered in .243 Winchester and 22-250.

Savage 10 XP Predator Hunter

Savage, long known for producing extremely accurate rifles at a fair price, jumped headlong into the predator hunting market with its 10 XP Predator Hunter rifle and added some super cool features callers will appreciate. The Predator Hunter is not just a standard rifle offered in smaller calibers. It was designed from the ground up with input from serious predator hunters regarding what they would like to see in a rifle designed for calling coyotes, fox and bobcats. The results are impressive. To begin, the Predator hunter is offered in several fantastic calibers, namely .223, .204 and .22-250, and sports a short 22-inch barrel for easy use. The synthetic stock uses dual pillar bedding for maximum consistency and accuracy and features an oversized bolt handle for operation with heavy gloves. The rifle comes also comes as a kit with a factory mounted and bore sighted 3 x 9 scope. The whole package is dipped in Mossy Oak Brush pattern. I spent several days testing one of these rifles in eastern Colorado and was extremely impressed with the overall accuracy (factory rounds regularly churned out sub-MOA groups), functionality and fantastic AccuTrigger system. After a few days and several hundred rounds, my only complaint with the rifle is the lack of option for an internal box magazine. From a predator hunter standpoint, I think the package would be improved upon with a detachable magazine, at least as an option.

Weatherby Mark V SVR

The Weatherby Mark V SVR (Short Varmint Rifle) is another high quality rifle built specifically with the predator caller in mind. It sports a short lighter-weight barrel than other varmint rifles as well as a thinner, lighter-weight stock. The barrel is a 22-inch button rifled, chrome-moly barrel with an 11-degree target crown. The grey spiderweb pattern stock is hand laminated composite with a CNC machined aluminum bedding block for precise, stable bedding for shot-to-shot consistency. It's topped off with a Pachmayr Decelerator pad. My test rifle out of the box had a fantastically crisp trigger, which was pre-set at the factory at around three pounds. While the trigger is adjustable, it should only be done by a qualified gunsmith or Weatherby service center. Unless other models vary considerably from mine, I highly doubt most shooters would have it modified at any rate. Available in .223

or .22-250, both come with the Weatherby accuracy guarantee. My test rifle at the range sailed easily under the factory warranty and regularly placed three shots under three-quarters of an inch at 100 yards. Accurate, lightweight and quality throughout, the Weatherby Mark V SVR is an impressive rifle for sure.

Mossberg

While not a true predator rifle, after seeing the new LBA trigger system I felt compelled to include the Mossberg 100 ATR into the rifle line up. For a predator hunter often sitting all day in freezing conditions this is a huge plus. We need accurate rifles and a top notch trigger is part of the equation. However, a super-light two-pound trigger feels completely different at the range in the heat of July than it does when the thermometer is in the single digits and you can't feel your fingertips. This is where the Lighting Bolt Action trigger system comes in. The design of the LBA offers a truly crisp, creep-free trigger, optimizing accuracy. The LBA trigger blade blocks the sear from releasing the striker unless the

The big story for Mossberg rifles *is the newly designed trigger system called the LBA (Lightning Bolt Action). It's ideal for predator hunters wanting a light, safe trigger that can be manipulated while wearing gloves.*

blade is fully depressed, even at the lightest adjustment setting. A simple twist of a standard screwdriver enables the LBA trigger to adjust from two to seven ponds at home by the users.

Combine this new trigger with a short overall 100 ATR rifle chambered in .243 with a 22 inch barrel and you have the makings of an excellent all around predator rifle that can also pull double duty when deer season rolls around.

Howa/Knoxx Axiom

Uniquely suited for the predator hunter, the Howa/Knoxx Axiom rifle is based on the Howa 1500 action with some predator-specific improvements. The first thing most hunters notice is the unique-looking stock, which is the Knoxx portion of the rifle. This recoil-reducing stock, though very effective, is not critical for the smaller predator calibers. While the recoil reduction is not necessary for most shooters, what is nice is the adjustable length and comfortable pistol grip fit.

Howa/Axiom, Camo

The Howa Axiom
is a unique-looking, precision rifle. It features a Knoxx recoil-reducing pistol-grip stock and completely free floated barrel.

This rifle is available in two barrel lengths (20 and 24) and multiple calibers. In the 24-inch model, .204, .223, .22-250, .243 and .308 are available. In the 20-inch model, shooters can only get .223 and .308. Either rifle can be had in all black or dipped camo.

The Howa/Knoxx Axiom is ideally suited for either bench rest shooting, varminting or predator hunting by providing an adjustable configuration for all shooting positions.

Single Shot Predator Rifles

There is a long debated campfire argument whether or not single shots make suitable predator rifles. To some they epitomize a graceful rifle with classic lines, easy-to-carry style and smooth contours. This group often argues that one shot is all that is needed and tend to consider with disdain hunters who think they need a rifle with followup shot potential. The other camp makes the claim that predator hunting is a sport where multiple targets often present themselves, so why limit your success to one shot?

I tend to fall somewhere in between with my position on single shot rifles. I do like their looks, accuracy, simplicity and portability. And while I have learned to reload them very quickly, it is still no where near as fast as a good semi-auto. For probably 75 percent of the time I hunt with a single shot I am completely satisfied, generally killing a solo coyote or bobcat with the one shot. The other 25 percent of the time, when I either miss a coyote or have multiple coyotes come in, I itch for a quick followup shot.

Really you either like single shots or you don't. If you like them, then you will probably end up hunting predators with one and find it suits your needs just fine. If you don't like them or have no preference one way or the other, then you will probably be better off with a bolt action or a semi-automatic, as either of these rifle types will do anything a single shot will do plus provide a quicker follow up shot. Bolts and semi-autos are every bit as accurate (if not more so, having a more rigid stock design), as a single shot and either, when working properly, is reliable. To address the single-shot aficionado's preference for lightweight trim rifles, with modern materials any rifle style can be had in a featherweight configuration.

There are however several areas where some single shots shine over other action types. The first is in terms of sheer economics. Some single shot rifles such as the H&R Handi-Rifle family are bargains delivering precise accuracy for a fraction of the cost of other types of rifles. The second is

> Some single shot rifles such as the H&R Handi-Rifle family are bargains delivering precise accuracy for a fraction of the cost of other types of rifles.

Since the Encore *is available in so many calibers and can be had in lightweight configurations it makes a very good caller's rifle that seems to be gaining in popularity every year.*

for training youngsters. I am a firm believer in making the first shot count and nothing teaches a novice to make that first shot count like the knowledge that there is only one shell in the pipe. In addition to making the first shot count, a single shot is generally regarded as a "safer" firearm as it is easier to operate by novices who may get confused whether a round is chambered or not, or in the heat of the moment may forget to put a safety back on after taking a shot. While there is no excuse for not safely handling a gun regardless of action type, mistakes do happen and with a single shot they tend to happen less. Finally, for hunters who want to wring the most velocity from a given caliber, a single shot may be a better platform since longer barrels can be used and still retain the same overall length as other models of rifle.

The T/C Encore *makes for a great predator platform if you like a single shot rifle. If you keep an extra round accessible and practice a bit, a follow-up shot is not much slower than with a bolt action rifle.*

Thompson Center Encore

Of all the rifles mentioned here, the Thompson Center Encore is probably the most popular. Due to ease of reconfiguration, this one platform can serve as a rifle, a shotgun, a muzzleloader or a handgun. With hundreds of calibers available and many different types of stocks, this is a factory rifle that a hunter can essentially customize at home. I personally own three actions and several barrels and regularly hunt predators with one of them. They shoot well, have good triggers (or can be made to have good triggers) and carry well afield. As mentioned above, occasionally I wish I was carrying my AR-15 when multiple coyotes crest the far ridge, but I have found with a wrist or forend mounted cartridge holder that reloading the Encore is not as time consuming as many think.

Ruger Number 1

Between 1966 and the present, the Ruger Number 1 has been produced in a wide offering of calibers, from .22 Hornet to 458 Winchester and about every caliber in between. This gun is also available in a variety of different models, including the No. 1A Light Sporter, which features a light contour 22-inch barrel and an Alexander Henry style forearm. The No. 1 S medium sporter is virtually the same in looks and style as the No. 1A, with a lengthier 26-inch tube. The No.1B Standard Rifle sports a standard contour 26-inch barrel. The No. 1 V Special Varminter comes without factory sights, but with a wide beavertail forend and a heavy 24-inch barrel. The No.

Some believe *that predator hunting is a sport where multiple targets often present themselves, so why limit yourself to one shot?*

1 H Tropical Rifle features a heavier contour 24-inch barrel to accommodate larger calibers like the .458 Winchester Magnum. The No. 1 RSI International Features a 20-inch barrel and a full length Mannlicher-style forearm. The No.1 K1B and No. 1 K1V are a slight departure from the classic Number 1 mold. Both of these models feature stainless steel barrels and actions and laminated wood stocks. These are virtually the same, but the K1B model features a standard weight 26-inch barrel and the K1V has a heavy 24-inch barrel. Both models reflect their respective Standard and Varminter parentage.

Regardless of which Number 1 you choose, if you are looking for a classy single shot rifle that can serve dual purpose as a woods rifle or an open country gun - and if you find one that shoots well – the Number 1 may become the rifle you reach for every time.

H&R Handi Rifle

Currently H&R 1871 offers several version of the Handi-Rifle, including models with hardwood stocks and blued metal, laminated stocks and heavy bull barrels, and synthetic stocked models with both blued and stainless steel. In addition to this already extensive line of rifles, there is also a synthetic stocked super light model that tips the scales at slightly over five pounds, which makes for a great carrying rifle.

Handi-Rifles are available in a large variety of calibers from .22 Hornet to .500 Smith and Wesson. Whether you are looking for a long range performer such as .243 or a heavy hitter like a .45/70 or the new .500 Smith and Wesson, there is sure to be a Handi-Rifle that fits the bill.

Since a single shot rifle can make such a great first gun for a youngster, a special Youth Model Handi-Rifle is available with a 2½-inch shorter stock in a choice of .223 Remington, .243 Winchester or 7mm/08 Remington.

CHAPTER 9

SHOTGUNNING FOR PREDATORS

I began predator calling long before I could drive and, like any youth, I was impressionable. After my first experience with a hung up coyote at several hundred yards, I decided that predator hunting was a game of precise shooting equipment and long range marksmanship. So a few years later I put together the "perfect" predator rifle. I was extremely proud of that heavy, bull-barreled Remington 700 VLS in 22-250 topped with a Nightforce 8-32 scope (which by itself weighed more than some of my complete predator rigs do today). With visions of shooting coyotes farther than the human eye could see, I did a trigger job to make it break clean at two pounds and bedded the action to the stock. This rifle was to be my "White Feather" rifle intended to reign long range death on coyotes.

With the right handloads, it put the first three shots inside a quarter of an inch at 100 yards, and the next two made a pretty-as-you-please five-shot group that went under a half an inch – it was a tack driver. Thus equipped I was convinced there would never be another coyote safe from my wrath. The first time I took this gun out I was overlooking an open glade of waist-high sage brush. After my first blow on the call, three coyotes erupted out of the sage less than 200 yards away and were on a dead run towards me. Shouldering the gun all I could see was fur. I had forgotten the scope on 32-power from a previous ground hog shooting trip. Cranking the scope down I tried to reacquire my targets. They were now around 75 yards away and still coming full tilt, dodging and weaving through the sage. Even at

8-power, with the heavy rifle sitting on a stiff bipod, tracking those coyotes was nearly impossible. When a coyote's body briefly flashed through the crosshairs I squeezed the trigger…and missed flat out! The other coyotes took off to all points of the compass never to be seen again.

Right then I realized that, while this rifle may be ideal for picking off prairie dogs at a country mile, it was not an ideal predator rifle. This is a big mistake many hunters make – confusing predators with varmints. Often, hunters use the term interchangeably when the two sports are actually vastly different. Varmint hunting, at least by my definition, involves shooting small grass munching critters – namely prairie dogs, groundhogs and ground squirrels – at long range, meaning 100 yards and further. Predator hunting involves all carnivores, but mainly coyotes, fox and bobcats, which are most often shot while calling and generally under 200 yards. While you can get a rare long shot on a predator, often when called they come hard and fast and the tool to deal with them needs to be equally fast.

While coyotes do occasionally hold up, over time and with experience I found that selecting the right stand location and knowing how/when to call are bigger factors to success than having a long range rifle. In fact, as I called and hunted brushier/heavily treed country, I soon realized that sometimes hanging up wasn't the problem, not stopping was. In a situation where a coyote makes a mad dash right to your feet, no rifle is ideal - I needed something faster and easier to point at close range. This is where a shotgun comes in handy. It is perfect for those times when the targets are up close and moving fast. When coyotes close the distance from rock throwing to spitting, a good shotgun shines. But not all shotguns and loads are created equal.

Whether it is Hollywood, overactive imaginations of authors or just plain campfire lore…there is a mystique surrounding shotguns.

**A dedicated
shotgun** *with
sights, short barrel
and specialty choke
is an excellent tool
for hunting predators
when they come close
and fast.*

It is commonly believed they can knock down a charging brown bear, will make up for poor shooting and are capable of cleanly taking game at ranges best left to rifles. These old wives tales are simply that...tales. Shotguns are not a cure for poor shooting, aren't capable of extra ordinary killing power and most of all are very limited in reach. All that being said, shotguns can work extremely well for predators when their limitations are heeded. Of course like everything else, some shotguns and loads work better than others. If you are thinking about carrying a scattergun to your next tight cover stand, take these factors into consideration.

Gauge

Unlike bird hunting where smaller gauges are better suited to smaller fowl and a lighter framed gun makes all-day carrying at port arms an easier proposition, predator hunters don't have these same requirements. First off, predator hunters generally take all the size they can get; this means 12 gauge in 3-inch and even 10 gauge. When it comes to physical size and overall weight, these larger gauge "magnum" guns generally are heavy, but since for the most part they are carried on a sling from stand to stand and then rested over a knee, size and weight are not nearly as critical as they are when bird hunting.

> On a relatively slow moving predator where shot stringing isn't as much of a factor, I have seen hunters do great work with smaller gauges not traditionally associated with predator hunting.

Keep in mind, however, that gauge has nothing to do with power. The pellets from a 20 gauge are capable of traveling just as fast and just as far in the same tight pattern as they are from a 12 gauge, but all things equal, there may not be as many pellets in the pattern, and at longer ranges this may be critical. This perceived effectiveness is even debatable as more pellets in a pattern really shine on small, fast-moving targets like waterfowl where shot tend to get "strung out" on swinging birds. On a relatively slow-moving predator where shot stringing isn't as much of a factor, I have seen hunters do great work with smaller gauges not traditionally associated with predator hunting. The main disadvantage of smaller gauges is the unavailability of suitable large shot size loads from the factory designed for predator hunting.

Barrel Length, Velocity and Choke

The more I talk to hunters the more I think that barrel length is the most misunderstood part of a shotgun. Many shooters think that a long barrel is required to get the maximum velocity and range from a given shotgun. This is not necessarily true. There is a point of diminishing returns, and it is far shorter than what is commonly believed. Of course we have all heard the stories of "grandpa's old 32-inch barrel long tom shotgun" that dropped geese out of the sky at 100 yards. While the theory of more velocity from longer barrels may have been true 100 years ago when black powder shells were being used and needed plenty of barrel to burn the powder fully, it is no longer the case with smokeless powder (and hasn't been the case for the last 50 years). Any modern load will burn completely in less than 24 inches of barrel and anything after that gets purely academic returns. The idea that a longer barrel threw a tighter pattern never has been true. When it comes to "tightness" or density of pattern, it's more a function of internal barrel dimensions and choke than overall length.

When setting up a shotgun *be sure to test various loads and chokes. Not all shotguns are the same and performance may vary drastically with different choke/load combinations.*

Pattern your shotgun on paper *so you know exactly how it performs with the loads you choose.*

A short barreled gun with a full choke will throw a tighter pattern than a long barreled gun with an open choke – it is that simple. If both short and long barrels are of the same choke there may be a slightly better pattern with the longer barrel due to the gradual length of the constriction, but not enough difference that will ever be noticeable in the field.

Aside from choke, another factor that often makes a tighter pattern is the choice of shell itself. Loads that are "square" (A shotgunners term for a payload of shot that is roughly the same length as it is around) or as close to square as possible will generally perform better than a longer shot charge. This is due to several factors, but mainly it's because a longer shot charge tends to compress against itself upon firing worse than a shorter one. When it compresses it deforms pellets which often end up as "flyers" well outside of the core pattern. For this reason, if you pattern shotguns on paper you may find that your particular gun produces

> A short barreled gun with a full choke will throw a tighter pattern than a long barreled gun with an open choke – it is that simple.

better patterns with a standard 3-inch magnum than it does with a 3½-inch load. This is another reason a 10 gauge is so effective. A 10 gauge can throw a load which equals the physical payload of a 3½ 12 gauge but in a much shorter (or square) charge.

Another factor for tight patterns and a plus for square loads is the number of pellets being deformed on the outside of the charge and turning into flyers. The amount of deformation has been severely reduced with the advent of modern plastic shot cups, but it still occurs. The shorter this length of shot is on the outside, the fewer pellets can possibly be deformed.

Choosing a Choke

Choosing a choke is something that you really have to try for yourself. In a perfect world it would be nice to buy a particular choke and get the exact pattern it is supposed to provide. But that is usually not the case. Each individual load and every shotgun is different, so finding one choke that works perfectly in your particular gun becomes a bit of an effort in trial and error. The best way to find out what works best in your shotgun is with the help of a large steel patterning board, a selection of loads and a shoulder pad. Spend the day at the range checking various choke/load combinations at various ranges to determine what combination works best. Doing this, I have seen some amazing things, such as full chokes shooting tighter patterns than extra full chokes, chokes completely "blowing out" a pattern producing a doughnut like effect, and

The Carlson Dead Coyote is one choice for a choke tube that provided tremendous results.

improved cylinder chokes that shouldn't be anywhere near tight
enough for predator hunting be just about right. The point is, you
really don't know until you give it a try.

That said, if you are looking for a starting point, use a full or xtra
full turkey choke combined with copper coated lead BB shot. With
some slight tweaking this combination works pretty well across the
board. More recently I have been using the Dead Coyote Heavy
Shot Load which is super heavy T shot out of the Carlson Dead
Coyote Choke tube and have been getting tremendous results.

Keep in mind I use these types of chokes if I am trying to wring the
most from a shotgun in terms of range.
However, many times I choose a shotgun
for use in cover so dense you can't see a
coyote until it is in your lap. In these set-
ups, 10 to 25 yards is the normal shooting distance. And most 10-yard shots
are not stationary ones, they are running
through a setup at full tilt. With a full or
xtra full choke your pattern is about the
size of a softball – better odds than a rifle
but still plenty of room to miss. For these
close range sets I prefer a more open choke, often using an improved
or modified choke to give me a larger margin of error.

> With a full or
> xtra full choke
> your pattern is
> about the size of
> a softball – better
> odds than a rifle
> but still plenty of
> room to miss.

Another handy choke I've been using more and more in recent
years is the TRUGLO adjustable choke. Based on the concept of
the Poly Choke of old, this is one handy unit. Like the nozzle on a
garden hose, it can be cranked open or shut down with a quick turn
of the choke. Test this choke on your particular gun to find which
settings work best for your desired applications. I find that I can
crank this one down and squeeze nearly 50 yards out of my Mossberg shotgun, then open it up and have a wide pattern for those
tight sets. Because of this versatility, I find myself using this choke
more and more.

Sights

For flushing birds, a simple bead works great. When it comes to
shooting predators at longer ranges, or even hitting them up close
with an extra tight pattern, upgraded sights can make a big differ-

ence. Luckily there are many choices available from manufacturers like TRUGLO who make a wide range of fixed and adjustable fiber optic sights perfectly suited for predator hunting. While attachment methods vary from stick-on models to units that clamp over a standard vent rib, one thing they all share is ease of use so even a non-gunsmith like me can mount one in minutes.

For those looking for something more precise than iron sights, several forms of optics may also work. The key when choosing optics, whether it is a red dot or a traditional scope, is field of view. The whole point of using a shotgun it being able to hit those fast moving, close range targets. A magnified scope is not necessary as the magnification reduces your field of view making fast target acquisition very difficult. Think speed and the ability to clearly see your target/aiming point in low light conditions and you will be on the right track.

A great option for predator hunters is the Burris Speed Bead. The heart of this sight is a small heads-up display red dot sight which they call their Fast Fire sight. The overall unit is tiny (one inch by one inch) which is nice as it doesn't add much weight or bulk to your shotgun, but what is really unique is

If your shotgun just has a metal bead *you may want to consider upgrading to sights with a red dot or fiber optic sights. Either choice will allow you to fine tune the point of impact and see better in low light conditions.*

The Burris Speed Bead *is a red dot holographic style sight. It is unique in that it sits low on the receiver and superimposes its red dot right over the standard metal bead. Should the battery ever run out or if you forget to turn it on, you can look through the glass and just use the metal bead as normal.*

the mounting base. Unlike other optics that mount above the action (i.e. above the rib of the shotgun), this unit utilizes a small base that attaches between the stock and the action superimposing the red dot right on top of the standard factory metal bead mounted on the rib. For fast shooting with optics nothing beats this system. Since most shotgun stocks are designed to work with the factory bead, anything mounted above the bead (a red dot or scope) forces the shooter to lift his cheek off the stock. Not only is this inaccurate, it is slower than simply mounting a shotgun and firing. With the Speed Bead system you can shoulder the gun as normal and the bead is instantly on target. Should you forget to turn the unit on or in the unlikely event that the batteries are dead (they run the unit for hundreds of hours) you can easily see through the small screen and use the metal bead as if you didn't have any optic attached at all.

Shotgun Loads

When I hear about coyotes getting bowled over at football field range, the skeptic in me kicks into high gear. Has it been done? I am sure it has, but it is a fluke. About half that distance is the maximum range you should engage a coyote with a shotgun and a quarter of that distance is even better. If you need to shoot 100 yards you need a rifle, not a shotgun.

For predators, *everything from 4 Buck to #2 shot can work, but the Dead Coyote T load stands out for predator hunting. It carries energy well and still has plenty of pellets on target to be effective.*

While coyotes, fox and bobcats have been successfully hunted with every load from OO buck to birdshot, I feel something in the middle of this wide range is a better bet. My predator hunting generally consists of one of several loads, including Winchester Supreme 4 Buck, Hevi-Shot "T" (Dead Coyote), and Federal copper plated BBs.

Shotguns kill by multiple, simultaneous impacts.

However, every pellet does have some energy and how it transfers and disrupts does affect total performance. It is my theory, when speaking of shotgun ballistics, that penetration is more important than sheer energy, for if the pellet doesn't get to the vitals, the energy it transfers is very miniscule. The ability to penetrate depends upon several factors including pellet size, hardness (malleability), weight and impact velocity. For this reason the copper coated pellets and hard shot go a long ways towards securing your game.

Awhile back I set up a test at the range with sheets of heavy paper cardstock roughly 16x16 inches square. I stacked up the card stock and fired at it with a variety of guns, loads and chokes from 40 yards. I then counted the number of pellets within a 12-inch circle and measured the number of sheets the pellets went through to get a comparative depth. After a day of testing and a bottle of Advil for the headache and sore shoulder, I realized that all of the loads I tested from 4 buck to number #2 lead would cleanly kill coyote-sized predators out to 40 yards. Past 50 yards none were reliable, but the 4 buck and T shot were the best performers. While it was a lot of work, it did show me that there really is no magic bullet when it comes to shotguns. When kept within 40 yards they are murder on predators, after that they become a lucky proposition.

A Custom Predator Shotgun
Without the Custom Price

It wasn't that long ago that if you wanted the perfect predator shotgun it meant several trips and a lot of money spent with a qualified gunsmith. Today, thanks to turkey hunters, this is no longer the case. In the last dozen or so years there has been an influx of highly thought out, custom tailored shotguns specifically designed for turkey hunting. Luckily for the predator hunter, the ideal turkey gun comes equipped with many of the features a predator hunter desires.

Most turkey guns are chambered in a magnum offering and feature a short barrel for ease of use. Some are pre-ported from the factory to reduce recoil/muzzle jump, which is a real benefit when shooting hard-kicking magnum coyote loads. Many are offered with synthetic stocks that work great in inclement weather and almost all are finished in matte or even camo finish to keep them hidden.

FEDERAl BB's
56 pellets
12" Circle
30 YARDS

Shotguns kill
*by multiple,
simultaneous impacts,
and are most effective
within 40 yards.*

Most turkey guns come equipped with, or can be fitted with, an extended xtra full choke tube and sport sights well suited to accurately placing tight patterns. Round off the whole package with factory installed sling swivels so you can easily attach a sling for long walks into the stand and you have a shotgun ready for everything from bobcats to coyotes.

Top Predator Shotguns

Mossberg

The Mossberg 500 Turkey, while designed for turkeys, is ideal for predator hunters as well. With full camo finish in hunter's choice of Realtree, Hardwoods, HD Green or Mossy Oak New Break-Up camouflage patterns, this gun will remain hidden from the wariest eyes. To make it even more effective in the field, Mossberg shortened the barrel from a standard 24 inches to a compact and easy to swing 20 inches. From my tests, this will not affect patterning or velocity in real world conditions one bit. Included in the package is Mossberg's new X-Factor turkey tube which has two rows of specially angled ports providing superior pattern performance and recoil reduction. While designed to fire tight loads of small diameter turkey shot, my testing on paper showed that it will also work with larger BB and T shot commonly used by predator hunters. Topping off the package are nice features such as factory-installed windage and elevation adjustable fiber optic sights, a drilled and tapped receiver for easy red dot or scope mounting, sling swivels and a thick recoil pad.

The Remington 870 Max Gobbler *is obviously designed with turkeys in mind, but it makes for a near ideal predator shotgun as well. Featuring a Knoxx Stock, full camo dip, extra full extended choke tube, sights and magnum performance, this gun will work wonders on predators.*

Remington

When I turned 13, the first shotgun I bought with my hard-earned chore money was a Remington 870 Wingmaster. It was used, had a fixed choke and plain barrel, and it only handled 2¾-inch shells. Back then 3-inch guns were sort of a rarity and for $149.00 I considered it the buy of the lifetime. After thousands of rounds, piles of birds and quite a few predators, my opinion hasn't changed one bit. The Remington 870 line of shotguns has been successful for one reason: They are quality firearms at a fair price.

While the 870 hasn't changed much in the last few decades, there have been some cosmetic modifications to the otherwise standard action, making it even better suited for the predator hunter. Take for example the 870 Super Magnum MAX Gobbler. It features a Knoxx SpecOps pistol-grip stock which has an adjustable length of pull and incorporates state-of-the-art recoil-dampening technology to tame the 3½-inch magnum loads. This is a really a plus on a pump gun. The 2¾-inch shells and even 3-inch shells are manageable, but without a recoil management system some of the hot new 3½-inch loads will pound you out of a gun. Other features include a 23-inch barrel with bright, fully adjustable Williams fiber-optic Fire Sights and a full dip in Realtree APG HD camo to keep it hidden. Unlike my original fixed choke 870, the MAX Gobbler has interchangeable chokes and comes from the factory with a Turkey Super-Full Rem Choke. While the basic function and quality haven't changed over the years, these refinements have made the 870 an even better platform for putting fur on the stretcher.

Benelli

I have been hunting with a Benelli off and on now for several years. Before owning one, I was skeptical about the reliability Benelli owners raved about. I own other autoloaders and, when fed the right ammo and kept clean, they perform well but are not without the occasional temper tantrum. But after hearing about Benelli's absolute reliability regardless of condition – dirty, wet cold, etc I had to try one for myself. After receiving the gun, I decided to make it a test gun. I wasn't going to clean it, oil it or for the most part take any internal care of it until it started to jam. I entered a trap league with it, shot random sporting clays events, turkey hunted and shot plenty of coyotes. Finally on a late Nebraska goose hunt where the wind was alternating between blowing icy snow and fine sheets of sand, it refused to eject a shell. By my count I had put over 2,000 shells of all types through it without a hiccup. I pulled the bolt out of the receiver in the field, wiped it off with my shirt, replaced it and it was right as rain again.

If you are looking for an autoloader that truly is reliable, you would be hard pressed to find one better than a Benelli, and the new Super Black Eagle II Turkey Gun is perfect for those with a predator persuasion. While the basic gun is the same as all SBEs, the trigger guard is now 30 percent larger than previous models, which is nice for hunters wearing gloves, and the whole gun is dipped in Realtree APG HD. Top it off with an action that is pre-drilled and tapped for a scope or a red dot and you have a ready to go coyote getter.

The Two Gun Approach

As much as I like shooting predators with shotguns, it is a rare day when that is all I take afield. It always seems that when I do, the odd coyote hangs up at 100 yards, refusing to take one step closer. For this reason I always bring a gun capable of reaching out and

Using a shotgun for a two gun approach is ideal. Keep the rifle in your lap and the shotgun ready for action. If a coyote hangs up, you will have ample time to lay the shotgun down and pick up the rifle.

touching a coyote that is past shotgun range. While I often carry a rifle, the burden of two guns gets to be a bit much, so often I strap my T-C Encore pistol in .243 to my pack. That handgun is capable of sub-minute of angle 100-yard groups and I wouldn't hesitate taking a 200-yard shot with it if I had the gun securely rested.

Regardless of whether I carry a handgun or rifle as a second gun, I always start my sets the same, with the shotgun across my lap in the ready position and the rifle or pistol rested next to me on a bipod or on my pack. If a coyote comes smoking through the set, a shotgun will greet him. If he holds up at 100 yards, I generally have more than enough time to lay the shotgun down and ready the rifle.

When you do enough predator hunting you will find that a rifle is not always the ideal tool for the job. Next time you head into timber or brushy country, consider giving a bird gun a day in court. You too may discover the magic of a properly used shotgun.

HUNTING PREDATORS WITH A HANDGUN

S ome folks scale mountains, some swallow swords and some get a kick out of climbing on the back of a bull and seeing if they can stay there for a few seconds. And some hunt predators with a handgun.

There are very few advantages to hunting predators with a handgun and a lot of hardships. However, it is a lot of fun when you connect, and it is this challenge that makes the sidearm so alluring and rewarding. By their very nature handguns limit your effective range; the amount varies by what type of handgun you choose. This means you have to be stealthier, watch your wind more carefully and spend more time at the range practicing than you would with a rifle.

The term handgun is pretty broad, and could reflect anything from a pocket protection piece to a bolt action affair that some would mistake for a sawed off rifle. The effective range for a handgun on predator-sized targets can be as little as 50 yards for a traditional hunting revolver with open sights to over 200 yards for a handgun with a longer barrel, chambered in a flat shooting cartridge and topped with a scope. The point is all handguns are not created equal, and selecting the "right" handgun to hunt with really depends upon how much self-imposed challenge you want to endure, as well as your own personal taste.

Handgun Types

For this discussion, I'll divide handguns into two main categories: short-range and long-range.

Short-range handguns are generally comprised of what most think of as traditional styled handguns. This can be a semi-automatic or a revolver (single or double action) with a barrel somewhere south of eight inches. This type of handgun can still be carried like a handgun, which is to say in a holster worn on the hip.

Long-range handguns are really more like short rifles than handguns. They generally have a barrel somewhere between eight inches and 16 inches and can be one of several action types, most commonly break open single shot or bolt action (either repeater or single shot). Most long-range handguns wear a scope to wring the most potential from their design, but many shooters prefer the easier to carry lines of an unscoped model. Long-range handguns generally give up portability and have to be carried either in a chest mounted scabbard or slung like a rifle with a sling.

Sights

When it comes to open sights, I prefer traditional black Patridge sights. In good light this style of sight provides a clean, sharp sight picture and incredibly accurate aiming point. For low light conditions some of the new fiber optic-enhanced iron sights are a great tool. While not as precise as Patridge-style iron sights, they do show up very well against a dark background – something that should be considered for normal hunting conditions.

When looking at aiming options other than iron sights, there are several varieties of electronic as well as traditional glass optics. Many shooters prefer red dot styles of sights, either the small holographic "heads up" display variety or the more traditional glass enclosed scope style. These sights have the advantage of only having to line up one sight plane with no magnification, which makes them very fast as well as easy to use for older eyes. In addition to working well, they are extremely compact taking up less room in a holster than a full sized scope. While they

Many shooters prefer red dot styles of sights, either the small holographic "heads up" display variety or the more traditional glass enclosed scope style.

Handguns can be used *in an ideal two gun set when hunting an area with a wide range of different sized predators. On this set in western Washington, coyotes, bobcats, fox, bears or cougars may be encountered. By using a small caliber rifle and a large caliber handgun, all the bases can be covered.*

are effective in speed shooting competitions, I have mixed emotions about them for predator hunting. To begin with, they often (but not always) require a battery. The disadvantage to this is that you have to turn them on right before the shot (which is just another thing to forget about) or leave them on and run the risk of the battery dying when you need it most. Also, since most are designed with speed, not accuracy, in mind, they make precise aiming difficult at longer ranges. While they may be right for some limited predator hunting situations they are not an ideal solution. That being said, of all the models I tried, I like the Nikon Team Realtree unit best. The dot size and intensity can be changed from a very large 10moa dot down to a tiny 1moa speck. This allows the shooter a choice between a precise aiming spot or an easy-to-see large dot during bright sunlight or against a snowy background. While this unit runs off batteries, I have found the usage to be very lean. In fact, I used it one full season without ever changing the batteries even though I left it on while in the field the entire time. It is a good idea to keep a spare battery in your kit just the same.

Scopes

For truly long range predator hunting a scope is a nice advantage. Handgun scopes come in many varieties from fixed power scopes in everything from 2x on up to around 6x, as well as variable scopes such as a 2x-7x or 3x-9x, with some models going all the way up to 12x. Like on a rifle, a scope allows the handgun hunter to see the target clearly, even in low light, and wring the most out of a long range handgun's accuracy potential. However, as good as handgun scopes are, they are not without their disadvantages. Since handgun scopes are designed to work with an extended eye relief, their field of view is substantially less than a comparative riflescope. This narrow field of view makes acquiring moving targets such as predators very difficult. Handgun hunters also need to consider the "shake" factor. The higher the magnifica-

> Handgun hunters also need to consider the "shake" factor. The higher the magnification, the more shake or movement is seen through the scope.

tion, the more shake or movement is seen through the scope. Keep in mind, this movement is always there – you just see it more with magnification. I would rather see it and control it to the best of my ability rather than try to ignore it with lower-powered optics. In addition to magnified shake, at higher power settings light transmitting is more severely impacted than on a traditional riflescope. For those two reason I encourage hunters to leave variable powered handgun scopes on their lowest setting, and only turn them up if you have a long shot at a stationary predator in plenty of light.

Choosing the Right Load

Choosing the right handgun load for predators can sometimes be difficult. Most traditional handgun calibers (.44 Magnum, .357 Magnum, .45 Colt, etc.) are loaded with bullets designed to penetrate larger game, not rapidly expand. Since most traditional handgun calibers have a pretty low velocity, rapid expansion is not always easy to achieve regardless of bullet weight or construction. Obviously this is not the ideal situation for predator hunters. Depending on the caliber, you may not have much choice when it comes to handgun hunting bullet selection. However, if you handload, a wide variety of custom offerings tailored to meet your specific needs are available.

> Since most traditional handgun calibers have a pretty low velocity, rapid expansion is not always easy to achieve regardless of bullet weight or construction.

In traditional, straight-walled handgun ammunition, such as the .357 Magnum, .44 Magnum, .45 Colt (and subsequent family i.e .454 Casull, and .460 Smith and Wesson), look for bullets designed with home defense applications in mind. These types of bullets are engineered to expand very rapidly, generally weigh less which produces a higher velocity and can work very well on thin-skinned predators. In addition to the more traditional, home-defense-constructed bullets, take a look at some of the newer bullets designed to fragment on impact for maximum expansion. For most predators this type of bullet may be ideal.

When it comes to long-range handgun cartridges, predator hunters will find much more suitable bullet offerings, since most long-range handguns can be obtained in common predator rifle cartridges. Most predator hunters using long-range handguns have them chambered in .17 Remington, 17 fireball, .223, .222, .22-250 or .243 Winchester. All of these cartridges loaded with lightweight expanding bullets will do the job just fine out of a handgun.

From Range to Field

One of the biggest transitions handgun hunters have to make is getting field-ready. While I can shoot nearly sub-minute of angle groups with a scoped T-C Encore off the bench, take me (or nearly anyone else) off the bench and you see groups open up dramatically. This is something not generally experienced with a rifle. From the prone position, either slung in or with a bi-pod, I can't shoot as well as off a bench but can still hold MOA with a rifle. With a handgun, especially a long range handgun, there is no field position that compares to the bench. That being said, some field positions are better than others and practicing them ahead of time will up your odds when a song dog closes the distance.

Prone

If you can get into the position and the terrain allows it, prone can be a deadly position with a handgun, but it is generally best to have a large pack or "bean bag" handy for getting the right elevation. While it is stable, the downside of prone is that it is pretty inflexible. As long as a predator comes directly down the pipe, you are golden. If he comes in off to one side, shifting around in time can be next to impossible. For this reason many predator hunters pick positions other than prone.

Creedmore Position

Long popular with silhouette shooters, Creedmore Position (lying on your back, gun arm extended along your upraised leg) is an accurate position, but one I am not overly fond of. It is hard to get into and the terrain generally doesn't allow for it. Even if it does, it is as unforgiving as basic prone if you have to relocate on a moving predator.

Sitting

In my opinion, sitting gives the best combination between flexibility and stability. When sitting, more often than not you can see above most tall grass and sage, but have almost the stability of prone. The basic sitting position I like to get into is with my back braced against some support – a tree, rock or even a solid fence post will work – then pull both knees up, about level with my chest. By bending both arms at the elbows I can comfortably lock my elbows into the hollows inside my knees for a stable but forgiving position.

Offhand

I really don't recommend offhand as a shooting position for either rifle or pistol hunters; it is just too unstable. Luckily for predator hunters it is a position rarely needed, as most of the time you are set up for the shot as you are calling an animal to you. The exceptions to this rule are when cougar hunting (shooting an animal out of a tree) or in the event you walk up on a wounded predator and it gets up. Since both cases are rare I won't go into offhand shooting technique much. Suffice it to say that proficient offhand shooting starts with a solid two handed hold combined with a solid stance. I prefer a modified Weaver, with my main arm (in my case my right) nearly straight and my off arm (my left) slightly bent, pulling ever so slightly back against the gun. Start with these fundamentals, then put thousands of rounds downrange and you will be on your way to proficiency. You will also likely agree that even when proficient you can do a lot better from some sort of rested position such as sitting.

Top Handguns for Predator Hunting

T/C Contender

The T/C Contender was one of the first modern long-range handguns seriously used for hunting. Introduced in 1967, it took the handgun shooting fraternity by storm with its extreme accuracy, versatility, ability to handle, (then) powerful cartridges and adaptability for a scope. The big attraction from the beginning, which carries through today, was the versatility. The frame's main function

Big-game guide
Dean Silva with a bobcat that he and the author called in one day to about 10 yards – well within handgun range!

is to house a single-shot barrel mounted with a single large pin. To change barrels, simply remove the forearm, drift out the pin and the barrel comes off. Put on a barrel of a different caliber, reattach the foreend and you are in business with essentially a "new" handgun. It's a pretty slick concept that is still in the forefront of T/C design today.

Over 40 years later, some refinements have been made to the basic concept, but there are many hunters, myself included, who still use a Contender for hunting and it works every bit as it did when it was introduced. While it isn't capable of handling the high pressure powerhouse cartridges the Encore and to a lesser degree the G2 are capable of handling, it still is available in more than enough calibers to get the job done adequately on all forms of predators, and it does so in a package that is considerably smaller, lighter and easier to carry than its bigger brothers.

T/C G2

The G2 is a modern rendition of the traditional Contender with some slight modifications. For one, the trigger group has been redesigned to allow for multiple cocking and uncocking of the hammer without breaking open the gun. This is an improvement over the original Contender which had to be broke if the hammer was let down before it could be recocked. Aside from the trigger group mechanism, the G2 took on some of the strength refinements of the Encore, namely beefier action sides to handle a wider range of higher-pressure cartridges. While not as big and heavy as the Encore, the G2 does weigh slightly more than the Contender. It should be noted that original contender barrels can be used with the new G2 action.

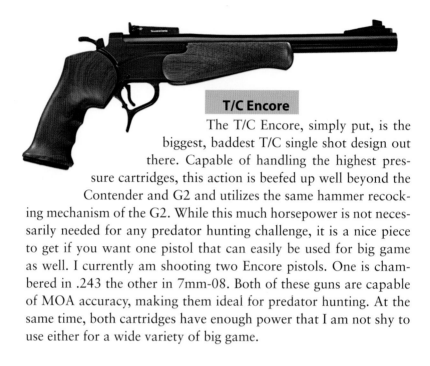

T/C Encore

The T/C Encore, simply put, is the biggest, baddest T/C single shot design out there. Capable of handling the highest pressure cartridges, this action is beefed up well beyond the Contender and G2 and utilizes the same hammer recocking mechanism of the G2. While this much horsepower is not necessarily needed for any predator hunting challenge, it is a nice piece to get if you want one pistol that can easily be used for big game as well. I currently am shooting two Encore pistols. One is chambered in .243 the other in 7mm-08. Both of these guns are capable of MOA accuracy, making them ideal for predator hunting. At the same time, both cartridges have enough power that I am not shy to use either for a wide variety of big game.

Smith and Wesson Revolvers

Smith and Wesson makes a whole host of revolvers in many different configurations. From the diminutive 17 HMR to the massive 500 S&W, they make a hunting revolver to suit about any need. This extensive line up of revolvers is further enhanced with Smith and Wesson's renowned Performance Center offerings, many of which are ideal for handgun hunters. From the Performance Center, I have some field experience with two that make ideal predator hunting rigs.

The first is the 460 XVR. There is no doubt about it, this is one massive handgun. The basis of this revolver is the mighty X frame, Smith and Wesson's largest platform designed to handle the 500 S&W cartridge.

Adapted to hold five of the fast-stepping 460 cartridges, this all stainless steel model sports a 12-inch tube for added velocity. Tipping the scales at 80 ounces, this handgun is physically large and in a large caliber, but it truly is versatile. Pushing a 200-grain bullet at 2,300 feet per second, this setup can work for predators up to and including large bears. After spending some time with this piece on the range, I can attest that it is a true tack driver. I was able to repeatedly print five shots under an inch at 50 yards with a scope with the handgun rested on shooting sticks; it will do even better than this off a sandbag rest. While this gun is large for general predator work, it would make a great dual-purpose handgun for hunters looking to cross over from predator hunting to big game hunting, or for mountain hunting where there's a good of chance of calling everything from fox to bears on one stand.

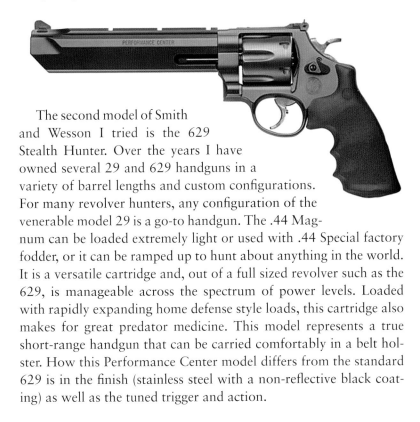

The second model of Smith and Wesson I tried is the 629 Stealth Hunter. Over the years I have owned several 29 and 629 handguns in a variety of barrel lengths and custom configurations. For many revolver hunters, any configuration of the venerable model 29 is a go-to handgun. The .44 Magnum can be loaded extremely light or used with .44 Special factory fodder, or it can be ramped up to hunt about anything in the world. It is a versatile cartridge and, out of a full sized revolver such as the 629, is manageable across the spectrum of power levels. Loaded with rapidly expanding home defense style loads, this cartridge also makes for great predator medicine. This model represents a true short-range handgun that can be carried comfortably in a belt holster. How this Performance Center model differs from the standard 629 is in the finish (stainless steel with a non-reflective black coating) as well as the tuned trigger and action.

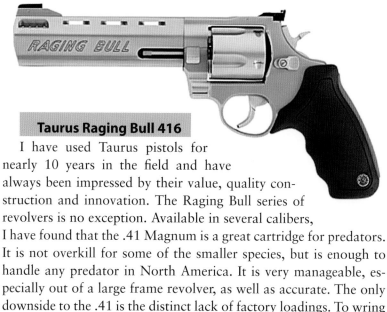

Taurus Raging Bull 416

I have used Taurus pistols for nearly 10 years in the field and have always been impressed by their value, quality construction and innovation. The Raging Bull series of revolvers is no exception. Available in several calibers, I have found that the .41 Magnum is a great cartridge for predators. It is not overkill for some of the smaller species, but is enough to handle any predator in North America. It is very manageable, especially out of a large frame revolver, as well as accurate. The only downside to the .41 is the distinct lack of factory loadings. To wring all the potential from this cartridge hunters would do well to handload. The mighty Raging Bull model 416 features a dual locking 6-shot cylinder with both the front and back engaged by physical locking mechanisms. This is a strong and stable system reminiscent of the classic Dan Wesson design. The 6½-inch barrel features factory porting to reduce muzzle rise, helping to tame this already tame load even further. For hunters looking to mount a scope atop of the Raging Bull, specific mounts are available to match this model's barrel. Like all Raging Bull models, the 416 carries Taurus Unlimited Lifetime Repair Policy.

HS Precision Pro Series 2000

Like the Remington XP100 and the Weatherby Pistol, the HS Pro-Series 2000 is a pistol based on a bolt action design. Generally very accurate, in my experience every bit as accurate as a rifle, these can be ideal for predator hunters looking for a long range handgun. From my field tests, the HS PS 200 lives up to its guarantee of 1/2-inch groups at 100 yards with the best three shot group I ever turned out from a bench – just slightly over .25 of an inch measured center to center.

The design of the HS is slightly different than most other bolt action pistols. It is a center grip single shot (versus a rear grip repeater) reminiscent of the early Remington XP100. While it has to be loaded with one shell at a time, I prefer this style of bolt action pistol as it reduces the overall length and brings the balance point much closer to the middle for better pointability. Available in a wide range of calibers, the predator hunter wouldn't go wrong with any of the following calibers: 223 Rem, 22-250 Rem, 243 Win, 257 Roberts, 260 Rem.

CHAPTER

11

THE REALITIES OF PREDATOR HUNTING

Not every hunt
*ends with fur on the
stretcher.*

I n talking to countless predator hunters over the years, two questions have come up time and time again. The first is, "I am not getting any response from predators. What am I doing wrong?" The second is, "I am starting to get the hang of this and have killed a few predators. What is the best I can expect to do?" While the number of predators available and the learning curve that goes along with predator hunting both vary, there are some constants.

A Slump and the Law of Averages

I think the biggest hurdle predator hunters have is working through the slow times. Slow times generally come in two forms. One is when you first get started in the sport and are learning about it. For most people, the time between picking up a call and actually calling in a predator is extremely long, especially if they do not have an experienced partner to accelerate the learning curve. During this time, they second-guess their sets, and are not sure how to properly make a stand, how long to wait, how long to call, what to look for in a good area, or how to source quality land. They often think they are not calling right, need better camo, or don't have many predators in their area. In fact, I believed for the longest time in my youth that calling must not work in Washington state as the only point of reference I had was Murray Burnham videos out of Texas. Well, I was wrong, Washington has plenty of coyotes and they readily come to the call if you know how to go about it. As it turned out, it took me several years to get the basics down.

This is typical for most novice predator hunters, and all I can say is you have to work through it. Hunt with as many knowledge-able hunters as you can, find more new spots than you can ever use and keep trying. Eventually you will wake up one day and realize you have a pretty good handle on predator hunting in your region. Much like a fly fisherman working a trout stream, it is not only important to know where a trout *will* likely be waiting for food, but also where he will *not* be. The latter comprises about 80 percent of a river. By automatically eliminating the unproductive 80 percent and concentrating on the productive 20 percent, your success will almost immediately increase.

The same is true for coyotes. Bad calling will often still intrigue a coyote into range, and you will at least see coyotes, even with an improper setup, and even if the coyote blows out before you get a shot. However, if you are not seeing any coyotes at all, it generally means there are few coyotes in the area and you need to find more productive land. Over time, you can figure this out pretty quickly by the "look" of the land combined with vocalization at night, scratch posts and droppings.

The second part of working through slow times comes when hunters become more seasoned. At this point in their hunting career, the hunter has a better understanding of predators and has probably called in a fair number of coyotes. Then all of the sudden the hunting goes cold or isn't as hot as they would like. This happens for many reasons, but is most commonly attributed to overhunting a prime area, educating predators to your presence, a change in food sources or simply the time of year and the conditions.

While it may appear that some hunters kill high numbers of predators either in print or on camera, the fact of the matter is they suffer dry spells just like anyone else.

In addition, there may be a misconception that some guys can piper up a predator at will. For the most part this simply isn't the case. While it may appear that some hunters kill high numbers of predators either in print or on camera, the fact of the matter is they suffer dry spells just like anyone else.

After hunting with a lot of expert callers from around the country, my experience has been that most hunters average around one coyote per four stands made – give or take a bit. This "one in four" rule is not a constant, but really an average over a season of calling in many different places. It varies by region and time of the year. There is no doubt that there are places in the West where the average is probably closer to one predator for every two stands made, and I would guess in the east or the Midwest the average is probably closer to one in six or seven.

Season after season I average around one in four stands myself, so when I have an exceptional day and rack up a string with better averages, I know somewhere down the line I will pay for it with a string of much lower calling success. The worst stretch I had was probably about one in 25 stands before we finally called in a coyote that we then didn't even manage to kill. The bottom line is, like a door to door salesman, keep telling yourself that the law of averages in on your side when you are going through a slump and that every cold stand just gets you that much closer to getting back to average.

When it all Comes Together

Often I am asked, "What is the best day, in terms of numbers of coyotes, a hunter can realistically expect." This is quickly followed up by, "What is the best day you have ever had coyote hunting?"

This is an interesting topic as really boils down why we hunt predators in the first place. It's for that one or two-day stretch that happens so rarely. It's when your free time, the weather, the moon and the seasons all collide to provide spectacular predator hunting. What a hunter can expect on these "best of the best" days really depends upon location. It's a simple fact that some parts of the country have more coyotes than other parts. If you are a hunter living in Wisconsin and hunt one of these great days, your potential may be a number of coyotes you can count on one hand. If you live in Texas, Arizona or many of the prime western states, this number may be in the teens.

What leads up to a best day? The best I have experienced have almost always been after a cold stretch of weather so nasty that hunting for food was almost impossible for coyotes. The longer the

Once they learn *how to call predators, the next question most hunters have is, "How many predators make for a good day?" Results vary by region, but in most places a couple of coyotes killed is considered a pretty decent outing.*

stretch of bad weather, the better the hunting when it finally breaks. Further, a break to extreme cold but calm can be better than a warm spell. If all these factors collide early in the year before the coyotes have been harassed or late in the year when they are starting to breed, that's even better. The final ingredient is the land itself. If you have access to large tracts of private land that have received little pressure, the coyotes will be ready to come to the call.

When all of these stars align with a day that you can hunt (and if you can't, you should try to make arrangements to do so – even if it means playing hooky from work) you will have an experience that will hook you on predator hunting for life.

I have probably hit one of these days every year for the last 15 or so years. They ranged in success from several dogs called in to in the teens, but they were all days to live for. However, my hands-down best of the best day took place during a tournament in Nebraska.

> The bottom line is, like a door to door salesman, keep telling yourself that the law of averages in on your side when you are going through a slump and that every cold stand just gets you that much closer to getting back to average.

My hunting partner was videographer and call maker Mark Zepp. We were hunting the panhandle of western Nebraska. The weather was in the teens throughout most of the day, getting down into the negative teens at night. The week before the tournament, the wind blew so hard that in order to walk you had to lean forward at a 45-degree angle. I was positive the coyotes had been holed up for most of that time.

The day before the tournament the wind stopped and the sun came out, but it was still cold. We went out on a scouting mission on a 20,000 acre ranch that hadn't been hunted in probably 15 years – we were to be the first in a long time. After driving around a bit, we quickly realized two things. First, there were tons of coyote sign. Second, we wouldn't be able to hunt all of this property in several days, let alone in a one-day tournament. With a couple hours of remaining daylight we decided to park the truck and make some test

The key to consistent, successful predator hunting is to keep making stands. There is always another dog somewhere over the next horizon.

calling stands on property we weren't going to get to in the tournament. In two stands we called up and killed three coyotes. Pumped about the following day, we organized gear and turned in early.

The next morning I got up a couple of hours before first light and made a stand behind my farm house, hoping to intercept a chicken coop-raiding coyote I had been saving for just such an occasion. Within 30 seconds of blowing on the call, a large male coyote busted out of the windrow less than 100 yards away. I hit him with a spotlight and one .223 bullet parked him his tracks. It was a great start to what would shape up to be a record day.

I met with Mark and had a quick breakfast before hitting our first stand site of the day. There was barely enough light to shoot

TIPS FOR BREAKING A SLUMP

• **Find a new area –** Sometimes things go cold because you've gone back to the well too many times. Find some new wells.

• **Switch up calls –** Like over-hunting an area, hunters get in a rut of using the same calls. Once a predator has been educated by a certain call, it gets tougher to call him in using the same sound. Switch up your call to switch up your luck.

• **Try a day of straight vocalization, no prey calling -** So many predator hunters use prey calls, so sometimes even switching to another call will not work: A different hunter may have educated a coyote with the call you are now using. Because few vocalize, you stand a better chance of offering a coyote a sound he hasn't heard before.

• **Go with a hunting partner to his spots –** Leave your spots alone for awhile and hunt a partner's spots. You get to see some new country and, more importantly, you may look at a setup differently than he has or may call it differently. Sometimes these little changes can lead to big results.

when the first coyote came sneaking in the back door. He saw us before we saw him, but I managed to kill him running away. The next stand also delivered a solitary coyote which spotted us and burned out before we could get a shot. The third stand of the morning was a bust, but the fourth stand brought in a pair, of which I got one. The fifth stand brought in a solo which I killed as well. The sixth stand looked like it was going to be a bust until we spotted three coyotes bedded 1,000 yards away by a yucca plant. No amount of calling would convince them to come in closer until Mark hit a lick on his pup distress call. They immediately all got up and came to investigate at a trot. A few

In some regions, *such as the heavily forested eastern United States, a single coyote in a day should be considered a success. Don't benchmark yourself against hunters from other parts of the country.*

minutes later, one lay in front of us while the other two high tailed it to safer parts.

We took a quick break for a late lunch and headed out again. The seventh stand was a bust, but the eighth stand produced a pack of three coyotes coming in at full tilt. I killed one when he stopped to look at us at 100 yards and clipped another on his way out of town. This second dog was wounded enough that we ended up using up the remaining daylight tracking him. We lost the trail when he got into the rocky hills, but as we watched the sun settle to the horizon, we knew we had just experienced "one of those days."

All in all we made nine stands and could have made ten if not for the wounded coyote. In addition, we were using valuable time setting up a video camera at each stand, and probably could have squeaked in a couple more stands had we not been filming. As for the number of coyotes, we saw twelve and killed six. Mark was armed with nothing more deadly than a Canon video camera, so we could have picked up a few more coyotes if he had been throwing some lead.

> Anytime I kill more than four or five coyotes in a single day I consider it a great day – the kind that only comes a couple times a year at best.

When you add in the three from the previous evening, we had killed nine coyotes in about a normal day of hunting. This was my best day of coyote hunting ever. I have heard stories of guys killing into the teens in one day, but I have not witnessed it. While I don't doubt their success, I will say they have to be a lot better shot than I am. Considering on any given winter day the average number of stands a hunter can make is between 10 and 15, this averages out to calling in and killing a coyote on every stand. Since this is highly unlikely, it means then that in order to kill over ten coyotes in a day, multiples have to be killed on some of the stands. Since I have only rarely seen a coyotes stand around after a shot has been taken, those hunters are probably connecting with some running coyotes. That in itself is no easy task. Like I said, I am sure it can be and has been done, but I guarantee it doesn't happen often.

Anytime I kill more than four or five coyotes in a single day I consider it a great day – the kind that only comes a couple times a year at best.

What Other Hunters Have to Say

Since the hunting around the various parts of the country is so different, I poled some of my predator hunting friends on the topic. I was curious to hear about their favorite spots, their best day and their longest stretch of nothingness.

Les Johnson

(Television host/executive producer *Predator Quest Television*)

Number of years predator hunting: I have been actively calling predators since 1989. I began to "try" calling coyotes prior to that, but would only try once or twice a winter using the old Johnny Stewart Record Player and didn't have much luck.

I have hunted, trapped, and tracked coyotes since I was 10 or 11 years old. My passion and obsession with outsmarting coyotes ultimately led me into just calling them. I shot my first coyote on the run with a .22 long rifle at about 75 yards.

Favorite place to call predators: I have called all over the western United States and in Canada. I love to call states that have lots of public land and those are the areas that I frequent the most. Wyoming, Utah, Nevada, Idaho, Oregon, New Mexico and Kansas, are some of my favorite states, but the Red Desert in Wyoming is probably my absolute favorite place to call. The Red Desert has very beautifully furred coyotes, lots of other wildlife (antelope, deer, elk, wild horses, etc) and tons of beautiful public land. The reason that I like the Red Desert the most is that it tests my ability of calling predators to the limit. The wind, weather conditions (very cold, snowy, etc) and vast size can make a weak man never venture out there.

Best day: Numerous times with another person (mainly my brother Jeff) we have gotten 12 coyotes in a day. I have per-

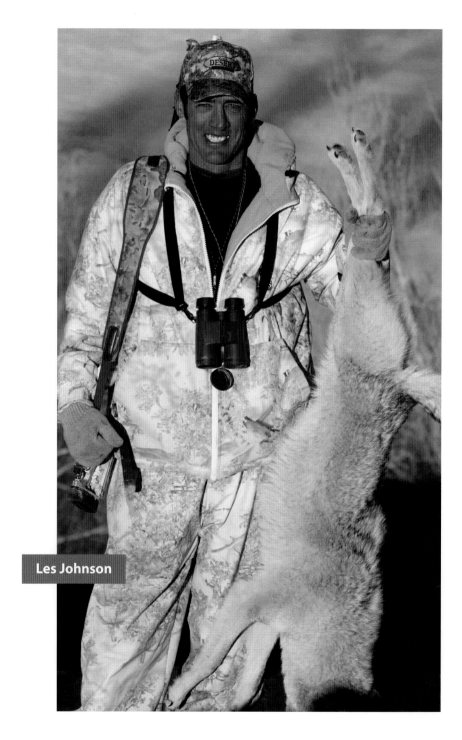

Les Johnson

sonally called and shot 11 coyotes in a day and had numerous eight and nine days. I have called and shot four coyotes on one stand, three with the shotgun. In Feb of 2006, my brother and I made a trip to southern Alberta to call and film for my television show. We called for seven days, and I had never been there before. My brother ran the camera and, in seven days of filming, we saw a total of 186 coyotes and I killed 46. It was the end of February. The first day I called and shot 11 coyotes.

Worst day or stretch of days: I had my worst success while calling in Wyoming during the middle of January. I remember a time in the winter of 1998 when I called more than 30 stands and never called a coyote. I remember seeing coyotes out on the stands, but they just sat out there and showed no interest at all in responding to my calling. These 30 stands accounted for seven to 10 different days of trying a few stands whenever time allowed.

When I first started calling coyotes, I remember making stand after stand after stand with no success. This went on from when I was 12 for four years. I was 16 before I ever called in a coyote. I'd venture to say that it took me 30 to 45 stands before I ever called my first coyote. I sit amazed at all of the testimonials that read "My first time ever calling and I called a coyote in less than 30 seconds!" This was never my luck, it took years of trial and error to figure it out. Maybe that is why I am so persistent at calling predators now, because it was so tough for me in the beginning.

Gary Roberson

(Owner of Burnham Brother Game Calls)

Number of years predator hunting: 45 years - I started when I was 10 and I turned 55 in March.

Favorite place to call predators: I have two favorite places: South Texas and Eastern New Mexico. I love South Texas for the sheer numbers; no place on earth with as many coyotes and bobcats. I love eastern New Mexico for the terrain. It doesn't have as many critters as South Texas, but it is user-

Gary Roberson

friendly, with lots of open and fairly easy elevation.

Best day: I don't remember the daily total, but three years ago I hunted for 2 1/2 days in South Texas and called up 68 coyotes. I was hunting with a good friend, Richard Hurt. Between the two of us, we killed 43 coyotes. If memory serves me correct, we had only two blank stands in the 2 1/2 days.

Worst day or stretch of days: In the shooting of Eyes Front III, Mossy Oak flew me to Alabama to hunt Portland Landing. There is no doubt that there are coyotes in that part of the world, but they were not there the two days I was. There was dog (actually hound) sign everywhere when I got there. I quizzed the fellow managing the property and he said that 37 Baptist Preachers had been camping and hunting coons for two weeks before I arrived but not to worry, for they left the day before. In the two days, I called in one gray fox. There is no doubt that the coyotes would be back, but they definitely were nowhere around when I was hunting. If they were, they were not making tracks and they were constipated. Cuz Strickland and I decided that we were not going to get blanked, so we loaded up and drove 150 miles to a big plantation. When we got there most of it was on fire (controlled burns). What was not on fire had grass taller than my waist. He hunted on it for one day and I went back to Texas.

Gordy Krahn

(Editor *North American Hunter*, TV host, past editor of *Trapper and Predator Caller magazine* and author of *Hunting Predators*)

Number of years predator hunting: 30

Favorite place to call predators: Arizona high desert on the outskirts of the little community of Congress. When I was editor of T&PC, Gerry Blair and I would pull his trailer out into the desert each January, park it there for a week and do nothing but trap and call fur. Coyotes, bobcats, lions, gray fox, oh my!

Best day: I think Gerry and I killed seven coyotes one day. The most memorable was a triple we called in and killed on the way back to the Phoenix airport. Gerry pulled off on a dim two-track and insisted we had just enough time to make one last stand. We could see them coming—three hard-charging coyotes—from a half a mile before they disappeared into the mystery of the mesquite and cactus. When they reappeared in single file at 30 yards, Gerry dropped two with his Ithaca 10 gauge and I took the trailer with the .243 Win.

Worst day or stretch of days: This happened just last winter on a TV hunt to the coyote-rich breaks of south-eastern

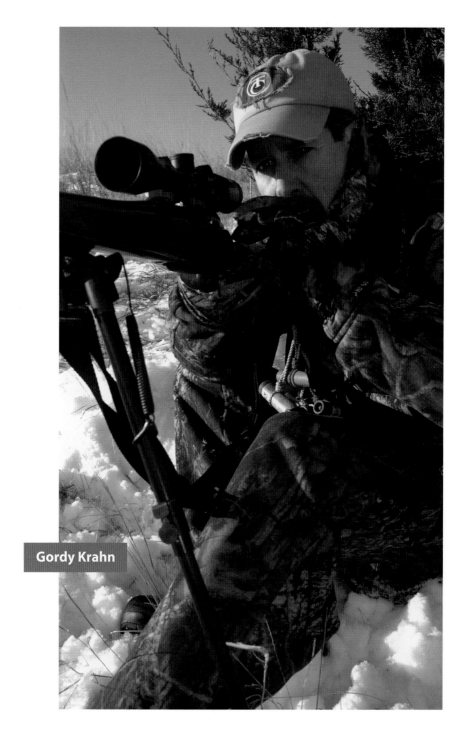

Gordy Krahn

South Dakota. I was hunting with you, Mike, and you as-sured me that putting a half-dozen or more kills on video would be child's play. Bad weather (40 mile-per-hour winds and driving snow) and bad luck (my choice of a hunting partner) conspired to net a big fat ZERO for three hard days of hunting.

Rich Higgins

(Dental laboratory owner and outdoor writer)
Number of years predator hunting: 42
Favorite place to call predators: I have no favorites. I enjoy the coyotes in the ponderosa forests as much as the coyotes in the low desert chaparral or Arizona. I love the diversity of this beautiful state.
Best day: 12 to 16 on one stand. All came in at once off a dead pile. Too many at one time and they came too quick to count accurately. Another time, my son and I called in 15 in a two-hour period and killed 14 of them. That was our best percentage. I called in 19 to the camera between 5:30 a.m. and 11:00 a.m. three years ago. What certainly was one of the most satisfying days was a hunt six years ago in which I guided Paul Wait, editor of *Trapper and Predator Caller* and a PH from South Africa, Lochi Lochner. We put seven coyotes in front of them on the first stand of the day. Paul was able to wring two or three magazine articles out of that one.
Worst day or stretch of days: My team blanked on a multi-club contest hunt four years ago. Many times we have blanked an entire day. All you can do is drive to a different part of the state and do better the next day.

Mark Zepp

(Predator call manufacturer and predator video pro-ducer)
Number of years predator hunting: 30 years
Favorite place to call predators: Staying single until I was

into my forties enabled me to hunt wherever and whenever
I wanted. Since I wanted to hunt just about every day and
had no family responsibilities, I spent several years traveling
and calling in all but two states west of the Mississippi River.
I prefer living and hunting out west, not because the coyote
numbers are better, but because the people numbers are fewer.
In my opinion, deer hunting has ruined much of the hunting
east of the big river. Most landowners don't have a problem
with anyone calling and killing coyotes, it's just tough to locate those landowners and get a chance to blow through a call
on their heavily posted properties.

After a lot of hunting and soul searching, I ended up in
southern Arizona. Other than west Texas, I believe we have
some of the best coyote numbers in the country. Of course we
have a lot of callers out here and there is a tremendous amount
of pressure put on these coyotes darn near year around anymore. So don't fly in or just show up and think you're going
to have the hunt of a lifetime. I've seen some big name guys
do this and head back home scratching their head with their
tail between their legs.

Best day: Fifteen years ago, outside of a subdivision north
of Scottsdale, Arizona, in the Cave Creek area, I once called
and easily counted 17 coyotes in two hours on a hot August
afternoon. These coyotes came in quick and easy and none
of them was over 75 yards away. Most were within 30 yards
and, because I wasn't carrying a gun and shooting at them,
they stayed around for a long time. They were in small 10
to 40-acre patches of ground located in between half million
dollar homes with golf courses close by. I didn't cover more
than two miles of ground. Night after night I went back into
those same areas and always called coyotes, but not like that
first trip. This was off of Scottsdale Road and even back then
it was a busy stretch of road. I traveled through that part
of the country last November while filming a TV show and
didn't recognize it. All of it has been covered up by housing
developments.

Worst day or stretch of days: My longest dry spell was
twenty years ago when I lived in Missouri. I had coyote fe-

ver bad back in those days, but working seven days a week made it tough to get enough time and quality stands in. I always made one, but never more than two stands before work from December through March. On one of the holidays, I made four stands in the morning and killed a coyote on each one of those stands, which is darn good in that part of the world. Then, I went 29 mornings in a row and never drew a hair or caught a glimpse of fur of any kind. Lots of crows and hawks, but no more coyotes. That's the stuff that makes you tough and keeps you going. No matter who you are or where you're hunting, you're going to have some dry spells. Stay optimistic, watch the wind and shoot straight when they show up.

Brent Rueb

(Owner of Predator Sniper Styx)

Number of years predator hunting: 30

Favorite place to call predators: Not to be funny, but where the predators *are*. What I mean is, there is no substitution for good scouting or paying attention to animal movements, listening to land owners and other hunters. I hate to have dry stands and the only way to get away from dry stands is to keep informed and pay attention to predator sign. I really like to hunt the desert type of terrain. We do not have this in my home state of Kansas so I try to hunt the high desert anytime I can.

Best day: My best day was hunting by myself with my two coyote decoy dogs. It was an early December hunt several years ago. We were out for two hours and took six coyotes. One stand was a double, two stands were singles and one great stand produced four coyotes. My best weekend was hunting with Dan Thompson in the Midwest Coyote Calling Event and we harvested eight coyotes. That was fun!

Worst day or stretch of days: Wow, this question is a tough one, as no one likes to say how long they have gone without calling in a coyote. But I do know that there was a

Brent Rueb

time that I hunted for a solid week and did not put any fur in the back of the truck. The coyote gods were not good to me that week. But there is always a red spot at the end of a dry spell!

Jamie P. Olson

(USDA Wildlife Services)

Number of years predator hunting: More than 20 years

Favorite place to call predators: If I can find a rough-cut leading away from the livestock or game animals, well that is were I am going to start looking for coyotes. I have hunted in coyotes in Texas, Arizona, Wyoming, Montana, Minnesota and North Dakota, and this always seems to be the type of area I trap, snare and call. Western North Dakota is where I learned to call coyotes. Give me a pasture or crop land at the foot of the badlands and I am all smiles.

Best day: My best day.....well I have had some great days hunting coyotes.

One time in western North Dakota a partner and I made

Jamie P. Olson

16 stands and called in 13 individual coyotes in one day. We split up most of the day and did most of the calling just walking through the area and setting up every quarter to half mile. We only covered about five square miles. In two and a half days of calling we had 25 coyotes come in on stand. It was late winter and we were blowing on howlers mainly using coyote vocalizations.

I have seen five to six coyotes come in on one stand many times and once had seven come in. While it looks cool, I would much rather have them come in one or two at a time.

While I have seen many coyotes in one day, I can't seem to break seven killed in one day. Now keep in mind this is all winter fur hunting. No decoy dogs or killing pup coyotes. With a partner, we have shot five or six coyotes a bunch of times and seven in day a couple of times, but never more than seven. Bad luck, equipment failure and misses have hindered us. Due to terrain and snow cover I can typically make six to eight stands in a day and, if I hustle, with good roads I can do as many as 10 stands.

In western North Dakota hunting early fall by myself, I started late and ended early (8 a.m.-3:30 p.m.) and made seven stands and shot five coyotes. I think that a typical good day hunting alone is three to four coyotes. Once in southern Arizona with a partner we had a day of calling in ten. We shot six and missed one. Another time in western North Dakota mid-February with a partner I called in 12 and we ended up shooting seven. We made eleven stands with lots of doubles in rough country with no opportunity for a followup shot.

Worst day or stretch of days: I once hunted in northern Arizona just off of the Utah border in late winter for three days. We only saw three coyotes while on stand. We got shots at two of them and only killed one. But it is not all about killing, we camped out with a couple of friends in a wall tent, saw some beautiful country and I would do it again in a minute.

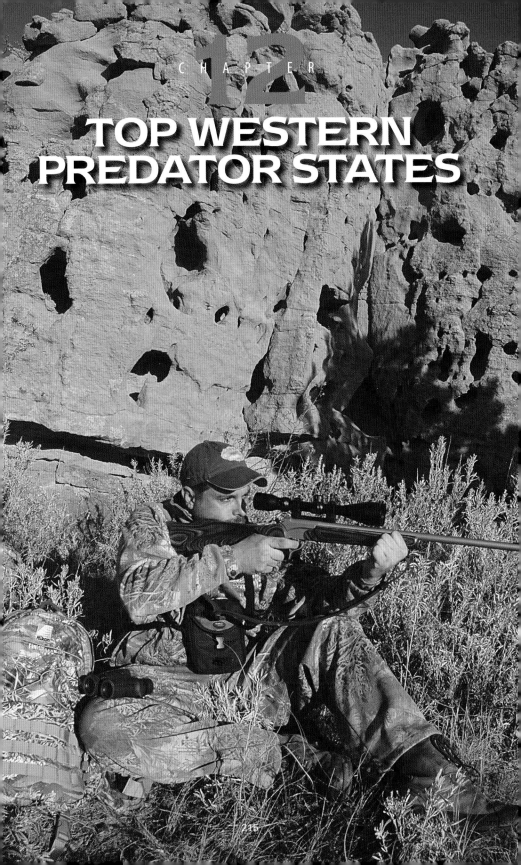

CHAPTER 12

TOP WESTERN PREDATOR STATES

This chapter contains information regarding predator hunting in various western states. Every state has different rules on seasons, license requirements, hunting hours and definitions of furbearers, non-game species and predators. Also, by the time this book goes to press some of the information (especially price and season dates) will have changed. So use this chapter only as a guide. It is not a regulation booklet or an official document of any sort. It is simply a guide to compare states and see what opportunities may await predator hunters interested in traveling across state borders. Before you hunt any state, read all the rules and regulations for the current year. If you have any questions, by calling the numbers listed below you can generally reach a state official with answers.

Arizona

Arizona Game and Fish Department
5000 W. Carefree Highway
Phoenix, AZ 85086-5000
602-942-3000
www.azgfd.gov

License
General Non-Resident Hunting License Annual $151.25
3-Day Small Game Non-Resident $61.25

Seasons
Coyote: Open statewide, year-round
Bobcat: August 1 - March 31
Fox: August 1 - March 31

Notes: Predatory mammals as defined by A.R.S. 17-101 are coyotes, bobcats, foxes and skunks. Bobcats are the only predator also classified as a furbearer with an export tag required to ship a bobcat pelt out of state. Tribal lands have their own regulations separate from Arizona State regulations.

California

California Department of Fish and Game Headquarters
1416 9th Street
Sacramento, CA 95814
(916) 445-0411
www.dfg.ca.gov

License
Nonresident Hunting License $134.95
Two-Day Nonresident Hunting License $38.85
One-Day Nonresident Hunting License $17.75
Bobcat Tags (Five) $13.25

Seasons
Gray fox: November 24 through the last day of February, statewide
Bobcats: October 15 through February 28, statewide
Coyotes: Year-round, statewide

Notes: Bobcats may only be taken under the authority of a hunting license and bobcat hunting tags as follows: Any person who possesses a valid hunting license may, upon payment of the fee specified in Section 702, procure only five revocable, nontransferable bobcat hunting tags. Such tags shall be acquired at designated department offices. These tags do not act as shipping tags as required in Section 479 for pelts taken under a trapping license. The holder of a bobcat hunting tag shall fill in his/her name, address, and hunting license number prior to hunting, and carry the tag while hunting bobcats. Upon the harvesting of any bobcat, the hunter shall immediately fill out both parts of the tag and cut out and completely remove appropriate notches that clearly indicate the date of harvest. One part of the tag shall be immediately attached to the pelt and kept attached until it is tanned, dried or mounted. The other part of the tag shall be sent immediately to the department. Shipping tags and marking are available from the department. All persons taking bobcat pelts under provisions established by the commission must personally present the pelt to a representative of the department for placement of the nontransferable tag or mark and shall furnish the following:

(1) Date of take;

(2) County of take and nearest major geographical landmark;

(3) Sex; and

(4) Method of take (trap, call or hounds).

The department shall mark bobcat pelts and issue bobcat shipping tags for export of pelts at designated department offices during the trapping season and for a 14-day period immediately following the trapping season.

An administrative fee of $3.00 shall be charged for the issuance of each shipping tag. There is no fee for marking bobcat pelts not for sale.

Colorado

Colorado Division of Wildlife
6060 Broadway
Denver, Colorado, 80216
(303)297-1192 (M-F 8am-5pm MST)
www.wildlife.state.co.us

License
Non-Resident Small Game Season $56
Non-Resident Small Game 1-Day $11
Non-Resident Furbearer Season $56
Non-Resident Youth Small Game Season $1

Colorado *is a fantastic state for predator hunters looking to take coyotes, fox and bobcats. While the whole state is good, the eastern half of the state may be the best. While mainly comprised of private land, permission is not too difficult to obtain.*

Idaho is a great state for predator hunters, but it can be a bit difficult to travel to and it is not as liberal as Wyoming for non-residents. Still there are plenty of predators and not a lot of pressure.

Seasons
Coyote: Year-round season state wide
Bobcat: December 1st – end of February Statewide
Fox: November 1 – end of February Statewide

Notes: Beginning April 1, 2009, all annual licenses including fishing, senior fishing, small game, furbearer, combination fishing and hunting, Colorado waterfowl stamps, habitat stamps and walk-in access permits will be valid April 1 through March 31 of the following year.

Idaho

Idaho Fish and Game
P.O. Box 25
Boise, ID 83707
(208) 334-3700
www.fishandgame.idaho.gov

License
Non-Resident Small Game $81.75
Non-Resident Nongame $29.25
Non-Resident Trapping $251.75
Youth Small Game (10-11) $7.25
Junior Mentored Hunting (12-17) $7.25

Seasons
Coyote: Open year-round statewide
Bobcat: December 14 - February 16 all regions
Fox: Open year-round in Southwest, Magic Valley, Southeast, Upper Snake, and Salmon Regions October 15-January 31 Panhandle and Clearwater Regions (see exceptions in notes)

Notes: No person may enter private land to hunt, fish or trap without permission if the land is either cultivated or posted with "No Trespassing" signs. Proper posting means either signs, 100 square inches of fluorescent orange paint or an entire fluorescent orange metal fence post every 660 feet around the property and at reasonable access points.

It is illegal to hunt any furbearing animal, except raccoon, with or by the aid of artificial light.

In Valley County and portions of Adams County, red fox may be taken only by trapping.

Fox are closed in Adams County on private land within the little Salmon River drainage.

Any person taking bobcat whether by hunting or trapping must comply with the mandatory check and report and pelt tag requirements by presenting the pelts of all bobcats taken to a regional office, the McCall office or official check point to obtain the appropriate pelt tag and complete a harvest report. To have a pelt tagged, the pelt must be legally taken in Idaho and must be presented to a regional office, the McCall office or designated checkpoint of Fish and Game during normal working hours - 8 a.m. to 5 p.m. A fee of $2.00 will be charged for each pelt tag. An additional $1.75 vendor fee will be charged to each license holder when pelts are brought in for tagging.

Kansas

Kansas Department of Wildlife and Parks
512 SE 25th Ave., Pratt, KS 67124
(620) 672-5911
www.kdwp.state.ks.us

License
Non-Resident Hunting Season $72.50
Non-Resident Hunting Youth Season $37.50
Non-Resident Furharvester Season $252.50

Seasons
Coyote: Open statewide year-round
Bobcat: Statewide November 12-February 15
Swift Fox: Statewide November 12-February 15
Red Fox: Statewide November 12-February 15
Gray Fox: Statewide November 12-February 15

Notes: No closed season for trapping or hunting coyotes. Motor

Like most of the Great Plains States, Nebraska has lots of song dogs. Non-residents are required to buy a somewhat expensive license, but if you are staying for a few days the cost is worth it.

vehicles and radios in vehicles may be used to hunt coyotes only. All furbearer hunting, trapping, and running seasons begin at 12 noon on opening day and close at midnight of closing day. Non-residents must have a furharvester license to hunt bobcat, swift fox, red fox and gray fox.

Montana

Montana Fish, Wildlife & Parks
1420 East Sixth Avenue
P.O. Box 200701
Helena, MT 59620-0701
(406) 444-2535
www.fwp.mt.gov

License
Non-Resident Trapper License $250 Valid October 15-April 15
Conservation License $10.00
Seasons
Coyote: Open season year-round statewide, no license required for non-residents
Fox: Non-Resident trapping license required to hunt fox
Bobcat: No open season for non-residents

Notes: Non-resident trapper licenses are available only to non-resident conservation license holders; 12 years of age or older, whose state of residence has nonresident trapper licenses available to Montana trappers. Valid for predatory animals and nongame wildlife.

Nebraska

2200 N. 33rd St.
Lincoln, NE 68503
(402) 471-0641
www.ngpc.state.ne.us

License
Non-Resident Small Game 2 Day $36.00

Non-Resident Small Game Annual $81.00

Seasons
Coyote: Year-round season statewide
Bobcat: December 1-February 28 statewide
Fox: November 1-February 28 statewide

Notes: Residents do not need any license to hunt coyotes. A habitat stamp is not required for coyotes for non-resident and residents alike.

Nevada

Nevada Department of Wildlife
1100 Valley Rd.
Reno, NV 89512
(775) 688-1500
www.ndow.org

License
Coyotes – No License required for non-residents
Kit and Red Fox - Non-Resident Trapping License required for hunting $192.00

Seasons
Coyotes: Open year-round statewide
Bobcat and Gray Fox : November 1, 2008 - February 28, 2009, Statewide, Closed to Nonresidents
Kit and Red Fox : October 1, 2008 - February 28, 2009, Statewide, Open to Nonresidents

Notes: Coyotes are an unprotected species in Nevada. They can be hunted by both residents and non-residents in the state without a hunting license. However, if you are selling the fur or trapping coyote, you will need a trapping license.

A person who holds a trapping license issued by NDOW is not required to obtain a hunting license to hunt coyotes, badgers, skunks, raccoons, weasels, ring-tailed cats or fur-bearing mammals.

Night hunting is not universally legal statewide, each county has their own regulations regarding discharging a firearm. If you plan to hunt at night, be sure to check the individual county's firearm discharge regulations.

New Mexico

New Mexico Department of Game and Fish
P.O. Box 25112
Santa Fe, NM 87504
(505) 476-8000
www.wildlife.state.nm.us

License

Non-resident trapper license $345.00
Non-resident small game $90.00
Non-resident, non-game $65.00
4-day nonresident small game $33.00

Seasons

Coyote: Statewide year-round
Fox: Statewide November 1st – March 15th
Bobcat: Statewide November 1st – March 15th

Notes: New Mexico classifies furbearers as either protected or unprotected. Coyotes are considered unprotected while fox and bobcats are considered protected. Nonresidents need to have a trappers license to hunt protected species, but for coyotes a nongame license or any current non-resident hunting license (including small game) will suffice. Residents do not need any license to hunt unprotected species.

North Dakota

North Dakota Game and Fish Department
100 N. Bismarck Expressway
Bismarck, ND 58501-5095
701-328-6300
www.gf.nd.gov

License
Non-resident fishing, hunting and furbearer certificate $2
Non-resident furbearer and Nongame license $25

Seasons
Coyote: Open year-round, statewide
Fox: Open year-round, statewide
Bobcat: Closed to non-residents

Notes: Nonresidents may not hunt on lands owned or leased by the North Dakota Game and Fish Department, including State Wildlife Management Areas (WMAs) and Private Lands Open To Sportsmen (PLOTS), for the first week of pheasant season (October 11-17). This restriction applies to all types of hunting, not just pheasants. This restriction does not apply to lands owned or managed by other state agencies that may be open to hunting, such as state school lands, federal lands that may be open to hunting, such as US Fish and Wildlife Service Waterfowl Production Areas (WPAs), or to private lands not enrolled in the G&F PLOTS program.

Oregon
Oregon Department of Fish and Wildlife
3406 Cherry Ave
Salem, OR 97303
(503) 947-6100
www.dfw.state.or.us

License
Non-Resident Small Game Annual $76.50
Non-Resident Furtakers License Annual $176.50
Bobcat Record Card $11.50

Seasons
Bobcat: Dec 1-February 28 Western Oregon no bag limit, eastern Oregon limit 5 bobcats
Gray Fox: November 15 through February 28 Statewide
Red Fox: Open season entire year for the following counties: Mal-

South Dakota
offers a variety of
habitat for the coyote
hunter. From the Black
Hills to the Missouri
River breaks to the
thousands of acres of
crop country, South
Dakota is a coyote
hunter's mecca.

heur, Baker, Harney, Morrow, Gilliam, Umatilla, Union, Wallowa and Wheeler; October 15 through January 15 in remaining counties
   Coyote: Year-round statewide season

Notes: Furtakers need only one license. A furtakers license allows hunters to trap, hunt and pursue. A hunting license for furbearers allows the holder to only hunt or pursue. A general hunting license is not required to trap, hunt or pursue furbearers. Juveniles younger than 14 years of age are not required to purchase a license to hunt or trap except for bobcat or otter.

South Dakota
South Dakota Game Fish and Parks
523 East Capitol Avenue
Pierre, SD 57501
(605) 773-3485
www.sdgfp.info
License
Non-Resident Predator/Varmint $40.00
Non-Resident Furbearer $250.00 (application needs to be submitted)
Non-Resident Small Game (will suffice for coyotes and fox) $110.00
Youth Small Game (will suffice for coyotes and fox) $25.00

Seasons
Coyote: Open year-round, statewide
Fox: Open year-round, statewide
Bobcat: Residents, December 13-February 15, Non-residents January 10 -February 15

Notes: Any person taking a bobcat must present the whole carcass and pelt to Game, Fish and Parks personnel for registration and tagging of the pelt within five days of capture. Non-residents can use a predator license or a small game license for coyotes and fox, a furbearer license is required for hunting bobcats. Applications for furbearer license are available from South Dakota Fish and parks

Texas *may be the quintessential predator hunting hot spot, as Realtree's Michael Waddell found out.*

headquarters in Pierre, SD.

Texas

Texas Parks and Wildlife Department,
4200 Smith School Road
Austin, TX 78744
(800) 792-1112

License
Non-Resident 5 Day Hunting $45.00
Non-Resident Annual Hunting $125.00
Resident and non-Resident Public Land Permit $48.00

Seasons
Coyote: Open year-round statewide
Bobcats: Open year-round statewide

Notes: Transport of bobcats out of Texas will require a CITES permit which is available at Texas Parks and Wildlife Department Offices. Call ahead before bringing bobcats in for CITES tagging.

Utah

Utah Division of Wildlife Resources
Box 146301
Salt Lake City, UT 84114-6301
(801) 538-4700
www.wildlife.utah.gov

License
Non-Resident Basic Hunting Annual $65
Non-Resident Small Game 3-Day $25
Non-Resident Furbearer $154
Non-Resident bobcat temp. Possession $5.00

Seasons
Coyote: Open year-round statewide

Washington State, *specifically the eastern half of the state, offers some tremendous predator hunting, from the Columbia basin to Hell's Canyon on the Snake River. Lots of private land but enough public to keep anyone busy.*

Bobcat: November 12- February 8
Red Fox: open year-round statewide

Notes: special regulations may apply on national wildlife refuges, Native American trust lands, and waterfowl management areas.

Washington

Washington Department of Fish and Wildlife
600 Capitol Way N.
Olympia, WA 98501-1091
(360)902-2515
www.wdfw.wa.gov

License

Non-resident Small Game $164.95
Non-resident Small Game, if purchased with a big game license $87.60
Non-resident Youth Small Game $16.43
Non-resident 3 days Small Game $54.75

Seasons

Coyote: Statewide year-round, however if hounds are used the season is September 2 - March 15th, except year-round with hounds in Adams, Benton, Franklin, and Grant counties.

Fox: Statewide September 2-March 15 (closed within the exterior boundaries of the Mt. Baker-Snoqualmie, Okanogan, Wentachee and Giford Pinchot National Forest and GMUs 407 and 410).

Bobcat: Statewide Sept 2 to March 15th

Notes: Bobcat pelts must be sealed at a DFW office. Be aware of the fox area closures, as they comprise very large tracts of Washington real estate.

Wyoming

Wyoming Game and Fish
5400 Bishop Boulevard

Cheyenne, WY 82006
307-777-4600
www.gf.state.wy.us

License
No license is required for non-residents to hunt coyote or fox

Seasons
The season for fox and coyote is year-round statewide.

Notes: Wyoming is one of the most cost-effective, regulation-free states for non-resident predator hunters. No license is required for hunting fox or coyotes, however a furbearer license is required to hunt bobcats. Nonresidents may obtain a trapping license in Wyoming only if their home state issues a license to Wyoming residents to trap the same species they intend to trap.

It should be noted that night hunting is legal in Wyoming for fox and coyotes, only so on private land with written permission.

CHAPTER

PREDATOR HUNTING THE DARK CONTINENT

Most predator hunters chase coyotes and bobcats because they love the challenge and enjoy the sport. But for many, the biggest draw is that predator hunting is accessible and affordable. In a world of expensive deer-land leases, guided western hunts, trespass fees and draw tags, predator hunting is still pretty simple. There is not a state in the west that you cannot hunt some kind of predator with an over-the-counter license nearly year-round. There are even a few states that welcome non-resident hunters with open arms, with no fee for a license for predators at all. It doesn't get much easier than that.

Maybe because of this, international predator hunting has not taken off in popularity among American hunters like it has with wing shooters and big game hunters. Be that as it may, from personal experience I can assure you that the allure of the predator's Siren doesn't stop at the United States border. Predators, in one form or another, exist on almost every continent of the world and, for the traveling hunter with a bit of an adventurous spirit, they can provide some unparallelled sport.

From fox hunting in Australia to coyote calling in Mexico and jackal hunting in the ranch country of South Africa one thing remains the same – the excitement of seeing a predator run into his next and hopefully his last free meal.

So if you ever get a chance, even if the purpose of your trip wasn't to hunt predators, be sure to throw a couple of hand calls in your carry-on bag. If you can rustle up a rifle from an old farmer, you might find that your hard earned skills as an American hunter will also pay off in other parts of the world.

Here are some places worth visiting.

Namibia

Africa is one big continent full of predators, most notablly the lion, leopard and cheetah. But these species are not what most traditional predator hunters go after. Their range is limited, the numbers severely controlled and the cost can be astronomical. When I think of African predators I think a bit smaller, namely the jackal, the caracal, the hyena and, with a stretch of the imagination, baboons, all provide excitement and sport.

I have been lucky enough over the years to hunt quite a bit of Africa's dusty and dry but beautiful real estate for many types of Plains game, some dangerous stuff and a whole truckload of predators. My Dark Continent wanderings have spanned a decade and have taken me from the Cape of South Africa north to Zambia, and down the mighty Zambezi River to the tropical coastline of Mozambique. But I started my African predator hunting sojourn in a country with an aptly named feature for a predator hunter: The Skeleton Coast of Namibia.

> My Dark Continent wanderings have spanned a decade and have taken me from the Cape of South Africa north to Zambia, and down the mighty Zambezi River to the tropical coastline of Mozambique.

Namibia is a harsh desert country bordered by the Kalahari to the east and the cold windswept Atlantic Ocean on the west. Throw in the Namib Desert (one of the driest places in the world) to the south and the (then) war-torn country of Angola to the north and you have a home for animals that is nearly untouched by human hands. There are a few hardy Germans who have carved out massive ranches working side by side with the indigenous Bushmen. Combine all of the people, natives, Germans, Afrikaans and English, and Namibia still is one of the least populated places on the planet. But what

Namibia lacks in people it makes up in game. And when there is game and livestock, there are bound to be predators. Because of this Namibia is also home to a burgeoning population of black backed jackal, fox eared jackal and silver back jackal.

If you have never seen a jackal, imagine a cross between a large red fox to small coyote. They tip the scales around 20 pounds and have a coat fit for a king. It is a lustrous silver, sooty grey and coal black combined to make an impression no other predator quite achieves. In the winter, which does get down to freezing in this desert environment, the hair gets as long and luxurious as a prime winter coyote in most parts of the United States.

> If you have never seen a jackal, imagine a cross between a large red fox to small coyote. They tip the scales around 20 pounds and have a coat fit for a king.

Like canine predators everywhere their diet is widely varied. They have been known to eat anything from ants to dead elephants, but most of the time they remain pretty satisfied with small rodents, rabbits and a little critter that looks like a mix between a rabbit and a kangaroo called a spring hare or "springhaas." The jackal is fond of livestock, especially lambs, and like the American West, if you can find a rancher with sheep and jackals, you will have a place to hunt quicker than he can say "Waidmanns Heil" (hail to the hunters).

My first encounter with jackals came when I was sitting in an elevated blind overlooking a waterhole, waiting with my bow for an unsuspecting kudu. A small duiker had snuck ever so quietly to the edge of the waterhole to get a drink before the fiery red orb of sun slipped below the horizon. I was watching the little antelope when I spotted movement of gray further back in the brush. My first thought turned to the gray ghost of the veldt, the Kudu, but within a couple of seconds I saw it was a jackal. The jackal was crouched low, slinking from bush to bush stalking the unsuspecting duiker. Normally I would have seized the opportunity and sent an arrow into the canine, but I was intrigued by the drama playing out before me. He got within 20 yards before the duiker realized something wasn't right. Before he could close the distance, the duiker lifted

Jackal *inhabit most of Africa and provide some excellent sport. They will come readily to the call and, for the most part, remain unpressured outside of the core ranching country.*

his head from the pool and with one quick bound disappeared into the brush. The jackal turned and followed. The duiker got away, as did my first opportunity at a jackal.

Upon arriving back and camp and telling the rancher of my sighting he chuckled and said in his heavy German accent, "Ahh yah me boy, Jackals are all ov'r this country, seeing one is not so special."

"Do they come to a call?" I asked.

With a puzzled look on his face he said, "I dan't know, but I've seen them come when ah' animal is ah' dying and crying out like a baby."

"Yup," I thought to myself, "they will come to a call."

A year passed before I made it back to the ranch, and this time I had several rabbit in distress calls tucked into my pack. I didn't know if African rabbits, spring hares and small rodents screamed like American prey, but I had to assume pain knew no borders. Besides it was the best I could do, at that time there were no calls I could find specifically for Africa. I went to a large, dry river bed and set up with the wind in my face, just like calling any predator back home. Within five minutes of blowing that call I spotted the silver sheen of a jackal working his way towards me through the thick brush. When he popped out into the riverbed around 75 yards away, I lip-squeaked and he stopped exactly like a coyote would, alert, peering for the source of the noise. I put the crosshairs on his chest and squeezed the trigger. Walking up to him, I was amazed at how gorgeous he was. Smaller than an American coyote, I would guess he weighed in the high teens, but his coat was long and full and simply magnificent.

I hunted jackals on and off for almost a year while working in Africa, and for the most part they respond like coyotes. They will come on the run to all manners of prey-in-distress calls, just like a coyote, and they vocalize as well. While I never mastered any form of vocalization with them, I am sure during the right time of year with the right call, they could be called in with female invitations or male challenge barks.

Since my last trip there I noticed FOXPRO has several African species, including jackal vocalization, in their sound library and I have had them added to my FX5. I am anxiously waiting my return to try out some new techniques.

South Africa

After leaving Namibia I went to South Africa to work for an outfitter for several months, and what I found there will excite any predator hunter. Imagine miles upon miles and hectare upon hectare of untouched rolling pasture land with expansive sheep farms. Where there are easy meals like sheep, native predators like jackal and felines abound.

South Africa may offer some of the best predator hunting on the entire African continent. Much like the United States, South Africa is comprised of large tracks of agricultural and livestock country. I have hunted several of these large ranches in the Drakensburg Mountains for caracals (also called rooicats, red cat directly translated from Afrikaans) as well as jackals. The number of predators is simply amazing. At night you can hear countless jackals yipping and calling back and forth and a short drive with a spotlight produces at least a few pairs of caracal eyes staring back from the inky gloom.

Much like the
United States,
South Africa is
comprised of
large tracks of
agricultural and
livestock country.

For American predator callers this type of country is easy to hunt. Much like the agricultural western U.S., there are large pasture fields, little scrub brush and enough change in elevation to make setting up easy. The biggest thing I found enjoyable about hunting predators there is the sheer size of the ranches. Getting on a ranch that is over 30,000 contiguous acres is pretty commonplace, and many ranches are much larger. You can spend an entire week on one ranch and never see all of it.

Furthermore, predator hunting is a true service to African ranchers. Unlike America where game department programs financially offset the loss of livestock to depredation and predator control folks lend a hand to control predators, African ranchers are pretty much left up to their own devices. For this reason, they are more than happy to have predator hunters come onto their ranches. Some will even pay for the service or at least put you up with room and board during your stay.

Zimbabwe

Zimbabwe lies directly north of South Africa. It is bordered by Zambia and the Zambezi river to the north, Mozambique to the east and Botswana and Namibia's Caprivi strip to the west.

In Zimbabwe you begin to leave the modern agricultural world and step back into wild Africa. From the top of the Zambezi escarpment to the Zambezi itself, not much has changed since white men first came to this land hundreds of years ago. There are few ranches and even fewer fences. Hunters can expect to hear lions and leopards in the night and see elephant at the waterholes. While jackals inhabit the country, the real game for predator hunters in this neck of the woods is the hyena. Often referred to as the poor man's leopard, hyena require every bit as much cunning and guile as the great spotted cats and can be had at a fraction of the price. Hunting the hyena is similar to leopard hunting, as it is usually done over bait. But they can be called, especially at night with a light. However, in the area we were hunting the use of lights was not allowed, so we choose to hunt them over bait.

Making a hyena set is a fascinating process. We took buffalo scraps, mainly large sections of ribs and leg bones and wired them about three feet off the ground to a tree. Then we constructed a blind roughly 50 yards away. The blind-making process is interesting in itself. It is designed more as a shield than a blind. It is about seven feet high and four feet wide. It is constructed out of a branch frame with cross sections lashed in places, then covered with leafy branches. A few shooting ports are left open in the front. Behind the blind a trail is cut out

Often referred to as the poor man's leopard, hyena require every bit as much cunning and guile as the great spotted cats and can be had at a fraction of the price.

of the brush to the nearest dirt path or road. The trail is trimmed of all brush and limbs and literally swept with brooms down to bare earth for a silent approach. The plan is to walk in from the main road to the trail and then get situated behind the blind in the pre-dawn darkness. More than likely the hyenas are on the bait and have been all night. When it gets light enough to shoot, a rifle is poked through port and the hunter goes to work. At least that is the plan – it only sounds simple in the writing, in reality it is far more difficult. I played this game for six days straight with not so much as a shot a hyena. Oh we got close, but not close enough.

The first morning, my hunting partner Mike and I parked the Land Rover a half a mile from the trailhead and slipped down the path wearing long pants, boots and sweaters, as the mornings were cold. We could hear the hyenas on the bait talking in their own brand of insanity and smiled as we knew it was all over but the crying. While still 200 yards from the blind, the chatter stopped and all went silent. We continued on to the blind only to wait until light to discover nary a hyena around. Oh they had been there, but they must have heard our approach.

The following morning, we went in on our bare feet wearing nothing but boxer shorts. Mike was convinced the swishing of fabric had given us away on the first morning, as the wind was right for our approach. It is hard to know true nakedness until you creep through the dense African jess bush barefoot and practically nude. Every

__Hyenas__ are a challenging animal to hunt. Whether baited or called, their intelligence level is way up there and they always seem aware of their surroundings. Not an easy predator to hunt.

step your toes feel for a puff adder, every branch that brushes by your rib cage is a mamba. This time we got into the blind and the hyenas were still whooping it up, fighting over the bones of the recently shot buffalo. The bones made an eerie cracking sound in the morning stillness. In the diffused light I could see vague outlines and shapes moving around the bait, but none distinct enough to warrant a shot. One more minute would have provided enough shooting light. Thirty seconds later there was one short woof and all went silent. Not another shape was seen.

The next four mornings were repeats of the last. Hyenas were on the bait every morning, gone exactly one minute before shooting light. I left Zimbabwe with a great cape buffalo and a wonderful elephant experience, but no hyena. Hunters often dismissively say they shot a hyena, but no one can tell me they are easy. I left with a newfound respect for the cleanup crew of the Zambezi valley, and relish the thought of going back to settle the score.

GEAR LOCATOR

FIREARMS

Remington
www.remington.com

Rock River
www.rockriverarms.com

Howa
www.legacysports.com

Winchester
www.winchester.com

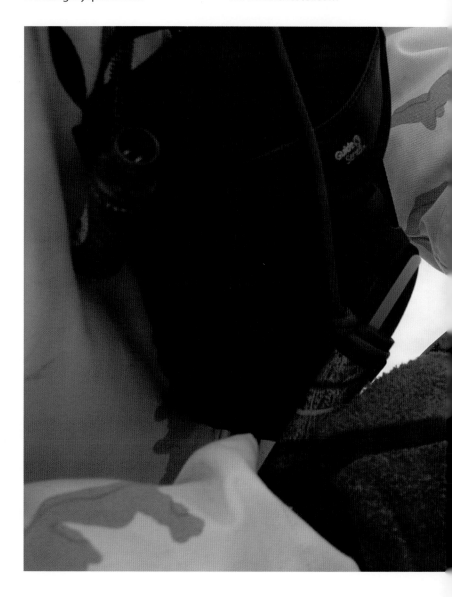

Weatherby
www.weatherby.com

Pyramid Air
www.pyramydair.com

Thompson Center
www.tcarms.com

Ruger
www.ruger-firearms.com

Kimber
www.kimberamerica.com

Mossberg
www.mossberg.com

Savage
www.savagearms.com

Smith and Wesson
www.smith-wesson.com

Benelli
www.benelliusa.com

CALLS

Zepp's
www.gamecalls.net

FoxPRO
www.gofoxpro.com

Snyper Styx
www.predatorsniperstyx.com

Dan Thompson
www.danthompsongamecalls.com

Hunter Specialties
www.hunterspec.com

Primos
www.primos.com

Burnham Brothers
www.burnhambrothers.com

Johnny Stewart
www.johnnystewart.com

RuffiDawg Calls
www.predatorquest.com

DECOYS

Flambeau
www.flambeauoutdoors.com

Edge
www.edgebyexpedite.com

Renzo
www.renzosdecoys.com

Mojo
www.mojooutdoors.com

Come Alive
www.tail-wagger.com

PACKS

Black's Creek
www.blacks-creek.com

Eberlestock
www.eberlestock.com

Kifaru
www.kifaru.net

Crooked Horn
www.crookedhorn.com

Blackhawk
www.blackhawk.com

Sitka
www.sitkagear.com

OPTICS

Nikon
www.nikonsportoptics.com

Swarovski
www.swarovskioptik.at

TruGlo
www.truglo.com

Bushnell
www.bushnell.com

CLOTHING/CAMO

Realtree
www.realtree.com

Whitewater
www.whitewateroutdoors.com

Scent Blocker
www.scentshield.com

Sitka
www.sitkagear.com

Filson
www.filson.com

SKINNING ACCESSORIES

Moyle Mink and Tannery
www.moytown.com

Fur Handling Equipment
www.nwtrappers.com

MISCELLANEOUS

Insight Flashlights
www.insighttechgear.com

Predator Pursuit DVD
www.predatorpursuit.com

Predator Quest DVD
www.predatorquest.com

The Trapper & Predator Caller Magazine
www.trapperpredatorcaller.com

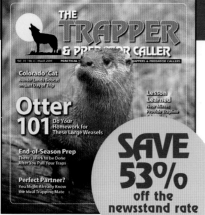

More Hunting How-Tos

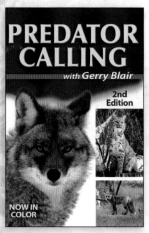

Predator Calling With Gerry Blair
2nd Edition
by Gerry Blair
Read the book today, and kill coyotes tomorrow. Using the proven techniques and equipment advice Gerry Blair delivers in this new edition successful predator hunting will be yours.
Softcover • 6 x 9 • 304 pages
200 color photos
Item# Z0740 • $19.99

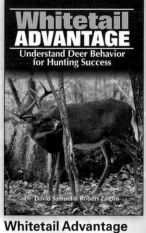

Whitetail Advantage
Understand Deer Behavior for Hunting Success
by Dr. Dave Samuel and Robert Zaiglin
Lean the basic biology of whitetail deer and apply it to make hunting season more successful than ever. Whether beginner or seasoned hunter, this guide has practical knowledge that can easily be put to use.
Softcover • 6 x 9 • 288 pages
100 color photos
Item# Z2227 • $24.99

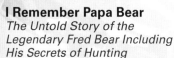

I Remember Papa Bear
The Untold Story of the Legendary Fred Bear Including His Secrets of Hunting
by Dick Lattimer
Discover pearls of wisdom from master outdoorsman Fred Bear as told through stories by his friends, including veteran rocker Ted Nugent.
Hardcover • 6 x 9 • 368 pages
125 b&w photos
Item# PPBR • $24.95

Do-It-Yourself Dream Hunts
Plan Like An Outfitter and Hunt For Less
by Mike Schoby
Arrange an affordable first-rate hunt using tips for legally accessing private land, using public land, getting a tag, transporting meat and trophy home, and explore a state-by-state guide to license costs.
Softcover • 6 x 9 • 256 pages
125 color photos
Item# Z1925 • $21.99

Krause Publications, Offer **GNB9**
P.O. Box 5009
Iola, WI 54945-5009
www.krausebooks.com

Call 800-258-0929 M-F 8 a.m. - 5 p.m. to order direct from the publisher, or shop booksellers nationwide and select outdoors shops.

Please reference offer **GNB9** with all direct-to-publisher orders

Order directly from the publisher at **www.krausebooks.com**